BOOK BY *Joseph Fields* AND *Jerome Chodorov*
MUSIC BY *Leonard Bernstein*
LYRICS BY *Betty Comden* AND *Adolph Green*

(Based upon the play *My Sister Eileen* by Joseph Fields and
Jerome Chodorov and the stories by Ruth McKenney)

Wonderful Town

A NEW MUSICAL COMEDY

RANDOM HOUSE, NEW YORK

WONDERFUL TOWN *was presented first by Robert Fryer at the Winter Garden, New York City, on February 25, 1953, with the following cast:*

(AS THEY SPEAK)

GUIDE	Warren Galjour
APPOPOLOUS	Henry Lascoe
LONIGAN	Walter Kelvin
HELEN	Michele Burke
WRECK	Jordan Bentley
VIOLET	Dody Goodman
VALENTI	Ted Beniades
EILEEN	Edith Adams
RUTH	Rosalind Russell
A STRANGE MAN	Nathaniel Frey
DRUNKS	Lee Papell, Delbert Anderson
ROBERT BAKER	George Gaynes
ASSOCIATE EDITORS	Warren Galjour, Albert Linville
MRS. WADE	Isabella Hoopes
FRANK LIPPENCOTT	Chris Alexander
CHEF	Nathaniel Frey
WAITER	Delbert Anderson
DELIVERY BOY	Alvin Beam
CHICK CLARK	Dort Clark
SHORE PATROLMAN	Lee Papell
FIRST CADET	David Lober
SECOND CADET	Ray Dorian

POLICEMEN   Lee Papell, Albert Linville, Delbert Anderson, Chris Robinson, Nathaniel Frey, Warren Galjour, Robert Kole

RUTH'S ESCORT   Chris Robinson

GREENWICH VILLAGERS   Jean Eliot, Carol Cole, Marta Becket, Maxine Berke, Helena Seroy, Geraldine Delaney, Margaret Cuddy, Dody Goodman, Ed Balin, Alvin Beam, Ray Dorian, Edward Heim, Joe Layton, David Lober, Victor Moreno, William Weslow, Pat Johnson, Evelyn Page, Libi Staiger, Patty Wilkes, Helen Rice, Delbert Anderson, Warren Galjour, Robert Kole, Ray Kirchner, Lee Papell, Chris Robinson

Production Directed by George Abbott
Dances and Musical Numbers Staged by Donald Saddler
Sets and Costumes by Raoul du Bois
Musical Direction and Vocal Arrangements by Lehman Engel
Miss Russell's Clothes by Main Bocher
Lighting by Peggy Clark
Orchestrations by Don Walker

SCENE

The play takes place in Greenwich Village in the '30s.

MUSICAL NUMBERS

ACT ONE

Christopher Street	Sung by Guide and The Villagers
Ohio	Ruth, Eileen
Conquering New York	Ruth, Eileen, and the Ensemble
One Hundred Easy Ways	Ruth
What a Waste	Baker and Editors
Story Vignettes by Miss Comden and Mr. Green	
	Rexford, Mr. Mallory, Danny, Trent, and Ruth
A Little Bit in Love	Eileen
Pass the Football	Wreck and The Villagers
Conversation Piece by Miss Comden and Mr. Green	
	Ruth, Eileen, Frank, Baker, Chick
A Quiet Girl	Baker
Conga!	Ruth
	Danced by The Cadets

ACT TWO

My Darlin' Eileen	Eileen and Policemen
Swing!	Ruth and The Villagers
Reprise: Ohio	Ruth, Eileen
It's Love	Baker and The Villagers
Wrong Note Rag	Ruth, Eileen and The Villagers

ACT ONE

ACT ONE

Scene I

(In front of the curtain, which is a semi-abstract impression of Greenwich Village, a GUIDE *and a group of gaping* TOURISTS *enter to a musical vamp in a style highly characteristic of the 1930s.)*

GUIDE

Come along!
> *(Singing in the brisk off-hand manner of a barker and indicating points of interest in a lilting song.)*

On your left,
Washington Square,
Right in the heart of Greenwich Village.

TOURISTS

> *(Looking around ecstatically)*

My, what trees—
Smell that air—
Painters and pigeons in Washington Square.

GUIDE

On your right,
Waverly Place—
Bit of Paree in Greenwich Village.

TOURISTS

My, what charm—

My, what grace!
Poets and peasants on Waverly Place—

GUIDE

(*Reeling off his customary spiel*)
Ever since eighteen-seventy Greenwich Village has been the
Bohemian cradle of painters, writers, actors, etc., who've gone
on to fame and fortune. Today in nineteen thirty-five, who
knows what future greats live in these twisting alleys? Come
along!
> (*As the* GUIDE *and group cross to the side, the curtain
> opens, revealing Christopher Street. The scene looks like
> a cheery post card of Greenwich Village, with Village
> characters exhibiting their paintings, grouped in a tableau
> under a banner which reads "Greenwich Village Art
> Contest, 1935."*)

GUIDE

Here you see
Christopher Street,
Typical spot in Greenwich Village.

TOURISTS

Ain't it quaint,
Ain't it sweet,
Pleasant and peaceful on Christopher Street?
> (*Suddenly the tableau comes to life and all hell breaks
> loose. An angry artist smashes his painting over the head
> of an art-contest judge who retires in confusion.*)

VILLAGER

Here comes another judge.

4

(A second judge enters, examines the paintings and awards First Prize to a bewildered janitor, whose well-filled ash can the judge mistakes for an ingenious mobile sculpture. The angry artists smash another painting over the second judge's head and all freeze into another tableau.)

GUIDE

Here is home,
Christopher Street—
Right in the heart of Greenwich Village.

VILLAGERS

Life is calm,
Life is sweet,
Pleasant and peaceful on Christopher Street,
(They freeze into another tableau as a cop comes in, a friend of the street, named LONIGAN. *He goes up to one of the artists, a dynamic, explosive character named* APPOPOLOUS.)

GUIDE

Here's a famous Village type,
Mr. Appopolous—modern painter,
Better known on this beat
As the lovable landlord of Christopher Street.
(Music is interrupted.)

APPOPOLOUS

(Breaking out of tableau. To LONIGAN—*violently)*
Throw that Violet woman out of my building!

LONIGAN

What's the beef now, Appopolous?

5

WONDERFUL TOWN

APPOPOLOUS

I'm very broadminded, but when a woman gives rumba lessons all night, she's gotta have at least a phonograph!

(*Music resumes.* LONIGAN *enters building.* WRECK *exits from building, carrying bird cage with canary. He meets a cute young girl named* HELEN *on the street. As they kiss the stage "freezes" again.*)

GUIDE

Here's a guy know as The Wreck,
Football professional out of season,
Unemployed throughout the heat,
Living on nothing on Christopher Street.

(*Music is interrupted. Freeze breaks.* WRECK *kisses* HELEN.)

HELEN

Hi! Where you goin' with Dicky Bird?

WRECK

Takin' him down to Benny's to see what I can get for him.

HELEN

Oh, no, Wreck! You can't hock Dicky!

WRECK

Take your choice—we either hock him or have him on toast.

(*Music resumes. He goes off.* VIOLET *comes out of building, followed by* LONIGAN.)

VIOLET

Let go of me, ya big phony!

(*Freeze.* VIOLET *drops valise on sidewalk, leans down,*

6

pointing angry finger at LONIGAN. *She carries large pink doll.*)

GUIDE

Here is yet another type.
Everyone knows the famous Violet,
Nicest gal you'd ever meet
Steadily working on Christopher Street.
(*Music is cut off.*)

VIOLET
(*To* LONIGAN)
Don't shove me, ya big phony!

LONIGAN

On your way, Violet.
(VIOLET *is pushed off by* LONIGAN.)

VIOLET
(*As she goes*)
You're a public servant—I pay your salary! So just you show
a little respect!
(*Music resumes.*)

ALL

Life is gay,
Life is sweet,
Interesting people on Christopher Street.
(*Everyone dances*)
Such interesting people live on Christopher Street!

A PHILOSOPHER
(*Enters, carrying a sign—*"MEETING ON UNION SQUARE")

7

WONDERFUL TOWN

Down with Wall Street! Down with Wall Street!
(*He freezes with the others, fist in air.*)

GUIDE

Such interesting people live on Christopher Street!

YOGI

(*Enters with sign* "PEACE")
Love thy neighbor! Love thy neighbor!
(*Another freeze.*)

TOURISTS

Such interesting people live on Christopher Street!
(*Two* MODERN DANCERS *enter.*)

MODERN DANCERS

(*Working hard*)
And one—and two—and three—and four—
And one—and two—and three—and four

TOURISTS

Such interesting people live on Christopher Street.

ALL

Look! Look!
Poets! Actors! Dancers! Writers!

Here we live,
  Here we love.
This is the place for self-expression.
  Life is mad,

WONDERFUL TOWN

Life is sweet,
　Interesting people living on Christopher Street!
　　(THE VILLAGERS *perform a mad dance of self-expression,*
　　which involves everything from a wild can-can to imita-
　　tions of a symphony orchestra. It works its way up to a
　　furious climax which ends with a last tableau like the
　　opening one, the final punctuation being the smashing
　　of yet another painting over the first judge's head.)

GUIDE

(Leading TOURISTS *off, as music fades)*
Come along,
Follow me.
Now we will see MacDougal Alley,
Patchen Place,
Minetta Lane,
Bank Street and
Church Street and
John Street
And Jane.

VALENTI

(A strange zoot-suited character struts in)
Skeet—skat—skattle-ee-o-do—

APPOPOLOUS

Hey, Mister Valenti, my most desirable studio is about to
become available, and I'm going to give you first chance at it.

VALENTI

Down there? *(Pointing to bars of a basement room below*
street level) When I go back to living in caves—I'll see ya,
Cornball.

9

(*There is a scream off stage and a kid rushes in, carrying a typewriter.* APPOPOLOUS *twists him very expertly. The kid runs off, dropping the typewriter.*)

EILEEN
(*Runs on*)
Stop him, somebody! He grabbed it right out of my hand! Ruth!
(RUTH *enters with two valises.*)

RUTH
(*To* APPOPOLOUS)
Oh, you've got it! Thank goodness! Thank you, sir. Thank you very much.

APPOPOLOUS
(*Pulls typewriter back*)
You're welcome, young lady.

RUTH
(*Holding out for case*)
Well?

APPOPOLOUS
Only how do I know this property belongs to you? Can you identify yourself?

RUTH
Identify myself?

APPOPOLOUS
Yes, have you got a driver's license?

RUTH
To operate a typewriter?

EILEEN

Now you give that to my sister!

APPOPOLOUS

How do I know it's hers?

RUTH

The letter "W" is missing.

APPOPOLOUS

Now we're getting somewhere.
(*Opens case.*)

RUTH

It fell off after I wrote my thesis on Walt Whitman.

APPOPOLOUS

(*Closes case*)

She's right. Here's your property. The incident is closed. Case
dismissed.

RUTH

Who are you, Felix Frankfurter?

APPOPOLOUS

(*Laughs*)

You can tell they're out-of-towners. They don't know me!

EILEEN

We don't know anybody. We just got in from Columbus
today.

RUTH

Please, Eileen, they're not interested.

HELEN

Columbus? That's the worst town I ever played in.

EILEEN

Are you an actress? (HELEN *nods*) That's what I came to New York for—to break into the theatre—

WRECK

Well, you certainly got the face and build for it—

APPOPOLOUS

(*Steps in to* RUTH)

And you, young lady, are you artistic like your sister?

RUTH

No. I haven't the face and build for it.

EILEEN

Don't listen to her. She's a very good writer—and very original.

RUTH

Yes. I'm the only author who never uses a "W."

(RUTH *picks up case and valise*)

Come on, Eileen. It's getting late, and we've got to find a place.

APPOPOLOUS

(*Laughing*)

Remarkable! You're looking for a place, and I got just the place! Step in—I'll show it to you personally!

RUTH

What floor is it on?

WONDERFUL TOWN

APPOPOLOUS

What floor? Let me show you the place before you start raising a lot of objections!

EILEEN

Let's look at it anyway, Ruth. What can we lose?

APPOPOLOUS

Of course! What can you lose?

RUTH

I don't know, Eileen—

APPOPOLOUS

What do you gotta know? (*He opens door*)
Step in. (EILEEN *steps through*. RUTH *follows*)
A Chinese opium den it isn't, and a white slaver I ain't!
    (APPOPOLOUS *steps in, closes door behind him*.)

VILLAGERS

There they go
Down the stairs.
Now they will live
In Greenwich Village.

Life is mad,
Life is sweet.
Interesting people living on
Christopher Street.
    (*They all dance off*.)

ACT ONE

Scene II

THE STUDIO: *A basement horror with two daybeds, an imitation fireplace and one barred window that looks out on the street above. It's a cross between a cell in solitary confinement and an iron lung.*

APPOPOLOUS

Isn't it just what you've been dreaming about?

RUTH

It's very nice, only—

APPOPOLOUS

Note the imitation fireplace—
　　(*Steps to bed, patting it*)
the big comfortable daybeds—
　　(RUTH *goes to bed, starts to pat it;* APPOPOLOUS *takes her hand away and points to window.*)
Look! Life passes up and down
in front of you like a regular parade!
　　(*Some people pass by—only their legs are visible.*)

RUTH

Well, really—

APPOPOLOUS

Let me point a few salient features. In here you have a model kitchenette—complete in every detail.

14

(RUTH *goes to door*—APPOPOLOUS *closes it quickly. He
goes to bathroom door. She follows.*)
And over here is a luxurious bathroom—
(RUTH *starts to look.* APPOPOLOUS *closes door quickly.*)

RUTH

They're awfully small.

APPOPOLOUS

In those two rooms you won't entertain. (*He indicates a
hideous painting on the wall*) You see that landscape? That's
from my blue-green period.

RUTH

You mean *you* painted that?

APPOPOLOUS

Yes, of course. This studio is merely a hobby—a sanctuary
for struggling young artists—and since you are both in the
arts, I'm gonna let you have this studio for the giveaway price
of sixty-five dollars a month.

RUTH

Sixty five dollars for *this*?

EILEEN
(*Weakly*)
Couldn't we stay here tonight, and then if we like it—
(RUTH *shakes head "no."*)

APPOPOLOUS

I'll do better than that. You can have the place for a month —on trial—at absolutely no cost to you!

RUTH

Oh, we couldn't let you do that—could we, Eileen?

APPOPOLOUS

And then, if you're not one hundred percent satisfied, I'll give you back your first month's rent!

EILEEN

(*Pathetically*)

Please, Ruth—I've got to get to bed.

(RUTH *gives her a look, sighs and starts to count out some bills.*)

RUTH

Twenty, forty, sixty-one, sixty-two . . .

(*There is a tremendous boom from below. The girls freeze in terror as* APPOPOLOUS *quickly grabs the money from* RUTH.)

APPOPOLOUS

That's enough.

EILEEN

My God!

RUTH

What—what was that?

APPOPOLOUS

(*Innocently*)

What was *what*?

16

RUTH

That noise—the whole room shook!

APPOPOLOUS

(*Chuckles*)

That just goes to show how you'll get used to it. I didn't even notice it.

EILEEN

Get used to it?

APPOPOLOUS

You won't even be conscious of it. A little blasting—the new subway—

(*He points to the floor.*)

RUTH

You mean they're blasting right underneath us?

APPOPOLOUS

What are you worrying about? Those engineers know how much dynamite to use.

EILEEN

You mean it goes on all the time?

APPOPOLOUS

No—no—they knock off at midnight and they don't start again until six o'clock in the morning! (*Goes to door and turns*) Good night—Sleep tight!

(*He goes out.*)

RUTH

Yes, Eileen—sleep tight, my darling—and you were in such a hell of a hurry to get to bed!

17

EILEEN

Ruth, what are we going to do?

RUTH

We're gonna do thirty days.
(EILEEN *exits to bathroom with suitcase.* RUTH *follows, looks in, and steps back in horror.*)
Thank God, we took a bath before we left Columbus!
(*She opens her suitcase and starts to take out her things. Woman with dog passes at window, dog stops and looks through bars.*)
Oh! You get away from there!
(*The woman and her dog go off.*)

EILEEN

(*Comes out of bathroom, combing her hair. She is in her pajamas*)
I wonder what Billy Honnecker thinks now?

RUTH

He's probably at the country club this minute with Annie Wilkinson, drinking himself to death.

EILEEN

He can have her.

RUTH

Don't you suppose he knows that?

EILEEN

And she can have him too—with my compliments.

18

RUTH

That's the advantage of not leaving any men behind—you don't have to worry what becomes of them.

EILEEN

Oh, it's different with you. Boys never meant anything in your life.

RUTH

(*Going to bathroom with pajamas*)
Not after they got a load of *you* they didn't.
(*She goes into bathroom.* EILEEN *sits on her bed and a moment later a man comes in the front door and calmly crosses to a chair and sprawls out on it.*)

FLETCHER

Hello. Hot, isn't it?
(*He offers* EILEEN *a cigarette.*)

EILEEN

(*Rising fearfully*)
I think you're making a mistake. What apartment do you want?

FLETCHER

Is Violet home?

EILEEN

No. No Violet lives here.

FLETCHER

It's all right. Marty sent me.

EILEEN

I don't know any Marty. You'll have to get out of here!

19

FLETCHER

Aw, don't be like that. I'm a good fella.

EILEEN

I don't care *what* you are! Will you please go!

FLETCHER

Are you sure Violet Shelton doesn't live here?

EILEEN

If you don't get out of here, I'm going to call the police! (*He laughs*) All right—you asked for it—now you're going to get it!
(*She goes to front door.*)

FLETCHER

Ha! They won't arrest me—I'm a fireman!

EILEEN
(*In the hall*)

Help—somebody—help!
(RUTH *comes out of the bathroom, stops in surprise as she sees* FLETCHER *and backs away.*)

RUTH

Oh, how do you do?

FLETCHER

Hello.

EILEEN
(*Comes in*)

Don't "how do you do" him, Ruth! He's nobody! (*She runs*

20

behind RUTH) He just walked in and he won't go away. Make
him go 'way, Ruth!

RUTH
(*Diffidently*)
Now you go 'way. And stop bothering my sister.

FLETCHER
No.
(WRECK *dashes in, still in his shorts.*)

WRECK
What's the trouble, girls?

EILEEN
This man walked in and he won't go 'way!

WRECK
(*To* FLETCHER—*who rises*)
What's the idea of crashing in on these girls?

FLETCHER
Now don't get yourself excited. It was just a mistake.

WRECK
You bet it was a mistake! Now get movin'!

FLETCHER
(*Goes calmly to door*)
Okay (*To girls*) Good evening— (*To* WRECK) You're the
hairiest Madam I ever saw! (*He runs out as* WRECK *starts after
him angrily.*)

21

EILEEN
(*Hastily*)

Oh, thank you—Mr.—

WRECK
(*Turns*)
Loomis—but call me The Wreck.

RUTH

The Wreck?

WRECK

That's what they called me at Trenton Tech. I would have made all-American, only I turned professional. Well, girls, if anyone busts in on you again, just holler. "I'm a ramblin' Wreck from Trenton Tech—and a helluva engineer—"
(*He goes off singing.*)

EILEEN

Ruth, I'm scared!

RUTH

It's all right, darling, go to bed— (*She leads* EILEEN *to a day-bed, then goes to fireplace and bumps her hips*) Aw, the hell with it! Let it spread! (RUTH *switches off light. There's no perceptible difference*) Didn't I just put out the light?
(*She pushes button again. Then, she pushes the button a third time.*)

EILEEN

There's a lamp post right in front of the window. Pull down the shade.

22

RUTH

There *isn't* any shade.

EILEEN

No shade? We're practically sleeping on the street!

RUTH

Just wait till I get that Appopolous! (*Sits on bed and winces*)
Boy! What Bernarr MacFadden would give for this bed!

EILEEN

Let's go to sleep.

RUTH

Maybe we can forget.

EILEEN

Good night—

RUTH

Good night—
(*A kid runs by window, scraping a stick against the
iron bars. It sounds like a volley of machine-gun fire.
The girls sit up, terrified.*)

EILEEN

What was that?

RUTH

It sounded like a machine gun!

KID

(*Runs by again, shouts*)
Hey, Walyo—wait for me!

23

EILEEN
(*Wails*)
Gee, Ruth—what I got us into.

RUTH

Oh, go to sleep!
(*Girls settle back wearily. Drunks are heard singing
"Come to Me My Melancholy Baby." They come up to
window, their legs visible.*)

EILEEN
(*Covering herself—shouts to window*)
You go 'way from there, you drunken bums!
(*Drunks stoop down, leering in.*)

FIRST DRUNK

Ah! A dame!

RUTH
You go 'way from there or we'll call the police!

FIRST DRUNK
Another dame! Look, Pete! There's two broads—one for you
too!
(*Wiggling his fingers happily at* RUTH.)

EILEEN
Ruth! Close the window!

RUTH
Me close the window!

24

FIRST DRUNK

No—the hell with her— (*To* EILEEN) *You* close it!

EILEEN

Ruth, please!

SECOND DRUNK

Don't you do it, Ruth!

FIRST DRUNK

Leave me in! I'll close it!
(*The cop's legs appear, nightstick swinging.*)

LONIGAN

What's goin' on here? Come on! Break it up! (*The drunks hurry away.* LONIGAN *stoops, looks in window*) Oh, I get it!

RUTH

I'm awfully glad you came, Officer.

LONIGAN
(*Heavily*)

Yeah, I'll bet you are.

RUTH

We just moved in today.

LONIGAN
(*Grimly*)

Well, if you're smart, you'll move out tomorrow. I don't go for this stuff on my beat. I'm warning you.
(*He goes off. The girls stare at each other in dismay.*)

25

EILEEN

Oh, *Ruth*!

RUTH

(*Goes to her dismally*)
Now, Eileen, everything's going to be all right.

EILEEN

It's awful!

RUTH

Never mind, Eileen—try and sleep.

EILEEN

I *can't* sleep.

RUTH

Try, darling—make your mind a blank.

EILEEN

I did, but I keep thinking of Ohio.
(RUTH *puts arm around* EILEEN.)

RUTH

Oh, Eileen— Me too.
(*They sing, plaintively.*)

BOTH

Why, oh why, oh why, oh—
Why did I ever leave Ohio?
Why did I wander to find what lies yonder
When life was so cozy at home?
Wond'ring while I wander,
Why did I fly,

26

WONDERFUL TOWN

Why did I roam,
Oh, why oh, why oh
Did I leave Ohio?
Maybe I'd better go home.
Maybe I'd better go home.
(*Music continues.*)

RUTH
(*Rises, defiantly*)

Now listen, Eileen,
Ohio was stifling.
We just couldn't wait to get out of the place,
With Mom saying—"Ruth, what no date for this evening?"

EILEEN

And Pop with, "Eileen, do be home, dear, by ten—"

BOTH

Ugh!

RUTH

The gossipy neighbors
And everyone yapping who's going with who—

EILEEN

And dating those drips that I've known since I'm four.

RUTH

The Kiwanis Club Dance.

EILEEN

On the basketball floor.

RUTH

Cousin Maude with her lectures on sin—

BOTH

What a bore!

EILEEN

Jerry Black!

RUTH

Cousin Min!

EILEEN

Ezra Nye!

RUTH

Hannah Finn!

EILEEN

Hopeless!

RUTH

Babbity!

EILEEN

Stuffy!

RUTH

Provincial!

BOTH

Thank heavens we're free!

(*By this time each is in her own bed, reveling in new-found freedom. There is a terrific blast from the subway below and they dash terrified into each other's arms and sing hysterically.*)

BOTH

Why, oh why, oh why, oh—
Why did we ever leave Ohio?

WONDERFUL TOWN

(*They cut off as music continues and go over to* RUTH's *bed, huddling together under the covers.*)

BOTH
(*Quietly and sadly*)
Wond'ring while we wander,
Why did we fly,
Why did we roam,
Oh why, oh, why oh—
Did we leave Ohio?
Maybe we'd better go home,   (RUTH: *O-H-I-O*)
Maybe we'd better go home.

(*They sink back exhausted as the lights dim. There is a fanfare of a bugle reminiscent of "Reveille," followed by the sound of an alarm clock as the lights come up sharply. It is early morning.*
RUTH *springs up as if shot from a cannon, turns off the alarm and shakes* EILEEN. RUTH *is full of determination.*)

RUTH
Come on, Eileen. Up and at 'em! Let's get an early start. We're going to take this town. Get up, Eileen!

(*She starts briskly toward the bathroom, suddenly winces and clutches her aching back, but limps bravely on. The lights black out.*)

(*There is a dance pantomime depicting the girls' struggle to get ahead in the "Big City" beginning with determined optimism and ending in utter defeat. Everywhere* RUTH *goes with her manuscripts, publishers are either out to lunch, in conference, or just not interested. Everywhere*

29

EILEEN *goes, looking for theatre work, she receives many propositions, but they are never for jobs. As the number comes to a finish the two sisters join each other sadly, collapsing glumly on each other's shoulders as the hostile city crowds sing to them "Maybe you'd better go home!" There is a blackout.)*

ACT ONE

Scene III

THE STREET, *same as Scene 1.*

ESKIMO PIE MAN

Eskimo Pies—Eskimo Pies—Eskimo Pies—
(RUTH *enters from house with milk bottles in a sack.*)

RUTH

Hey, Eskimo Pies! Will you take five milk bottles? You can
cash them in on the corner!

ESKIMO PIE MAN

I got no time for milk bottles!
(*He goes.* RUTH *puts bottles down.*)

EILEEN

(*Enters with a large paper bag*)
Be careful, Ruth—they're valuable!

RUTH

(*Wearily*)
Oh, hello, Eileen. What have you got in the bag?

EILEEN

Food.

RUTH
(*Eagerly*)
Food? Let's see! Where'd you get it?
(*They sit on the stoop.*)

EILEEN
At the food show. I saw people coming out with big bags
of samples. So I went in, and I met the nicest boy. He was the
floor manager—

RUTH
(*Nods sagely*)
Oh, the floor manager—

EILEEN
He loaded me up! We've got enough junk here for a week.

RUTH
(*Taking out small boxes of cereal*)
"Pep-O," "Rough-O," "Vita-Bran," "Nature's Broom." We're
going to have breakfast all day long.

EILEEN
It's good for you—it's roughage.

RUTH
I'd like to vary it with a little smoothage—like a steak!
(*Puts stuff back in bag.* VALENTI *enters and crosses, snapping his fingers in rhythm.*)

VALENTI
Skeet—skat—skattle-o-do—

EILEEN

Oh, hello, Mr. Valenti!

VALENTI

Hi yah, gate! I got my eye on you! *Solid.*
Skeet—skat—skattle-e-o-do—

RUTH

Who was *that*?

EILEEN

That's Speedy Valenti! He runs that advanced night club—
the Village Vortex. He's a very interesting boy. He had a cow
and he studied dairy farming at Rutgers and then got into the
night-club business.

RUTH

Naturally.

EILEEN

I auditioned for him this morning.

RUTH

You did? How'd he like it?

EILEEN

He said I should get myself a reputation and he'd give me
a trial.

(HELEN *and* WRECK *enter.*)

HELEN

Oh, girls! Can we see you a minute?

RUTH

Sure, Mrs. Loomis—what is it?

HELEN

Well, this is awfully embarrassing—I don't know how to tell you—

WRECK

It's like this. Helen got a wire that her old lady is coming on, which kind of straight-arms me into the alley.

RUTH

Haven't you room?

WRECK

You see, Helen's mother doesn't know about me.

EILEEN

You mean she doesn't know that you're married?

WRECK

Well, you might go a little deeper than that. She doesn't even know we're engaged.

(RUTH *looks at* EILEEN.)

HELEN

So, while Mother's in town we thought you wouldn't mind putting The Wreck up in your kitchen?

EILEEN

What?

34

RUTH

You mean *sleep* in our kitchen?

HELEN

You'd feel a lot safer with The Wreck around. And he's awful handy. He can clean up and he irons swell.

WRECK

But no washing—that's woman's work.

EILEEN

Well, maybe we could do it for one night, but—

RUTH

Wait a minute—

HELEN

Oh, thank you, girls. You don't know how much you're helping us out!
(*She goes.*)

RUTH

But, look—we haven't—

WRECK
(*Quickly*)

Gee, that's swell! (*Follows her*) I'll get my stuff together right away!

RUTH
(*Grimly*)

Something tells me you weren't quite ready to leave Columbus.

35

EILEEN

(*Smiles guiltily and goes to door*)

Coming in?

RUTH

No. I'm taking these stories down to the *Manhatter*— (*Holding up envelope with manuscript*) and I'm going to camp beside the water cooler till that editor talks to me.

See you later—

EILEEN

I won't be here later. I've got a date.

RUTH

With whom?

EILEEN

Frank Lippencott.

RUTH

Who's Frank Lippencott?

EILEEN

Didn't I tell you about the boy who manages the Walgreen drugstore on 44th Street?

RUTH

No.

EILEEN

He hasn't let me pay a single lunch check since I've been going there. Today I had a pimento sandwich, a tomato surprise, and a giant double malt—with marble cake.

RUTH

That's right, dear—keep your strength up. You're eating for two now.

WONDERFUL TOWN

EILEEN

I want you to meet him, so when *you're* in the neighborhood, you can have your lunches there too.

RUTH

Gee, since I've been in New York, I only met one man, and he said, "Why the hell don't you look where you're going?" (*Shrugs*) Maybe it's just as well. Every time I meet one I gum it up. I'm the world's leading expert on discouraging men. I ought to write a book about it. "Girls, are you constantly bothered by the cloying attentions of the male sex? Well, here's the solution for you. Get Ruth Sherwood's new best-seller—'One Hundred Easy Ways to Lose a Man.'"

(EILEEN *laughs and goes into house as* RUTH *sings in a spirit of rueful self-mockery.*)

Chapter one—

Now the first way to lose a man—

(*Sings with exaggerated romanticism*)

You've met a charming fellow and you're out for a spin.

The motor fails and he just wears a helpless grin—

Don't bat your eyes and say, "What a romantic spot we're in."

(*Spoken flatly*)

Just get out, crawl under the car, tell him it's the gasket and fix it in two seconds flat with a bobby pin.

That's a good way to lose a man—

(*Sung*)

He takes you to the baseball game.

You sit knee to knee—

He says, "The next man up at bat will bunt, you'll see."

37

Don't say, "Oooh, what's a bunt? This game's too hard for
little me."
(*Spoken*)
Just say, "Bunt? Are you nuts?!! With one out and two men
on base, and a left-handed batter coming up, you'll walk
right into a triple play just like it happened in the fifth game
of the World Series in 1923."
(*Sung*)
That's a sure way to lose a man.

A sure sure sure sure way to lose a man,
A splendid way to lose a man—
Just throw your knowledge in his face
He'll never try for second base.
Ninety-eight ways to go.

The third way to lose a man—
The life-guard at the beach that all the girlies adore
Swims bravely out to save you through the ocean's roar.
Don't say, "Oh, thanks, I would have drowned in just one
second more"—
(*Spoken*)
Just push his head under water and yell, "Last one in is a
rotten egg" and race him back to shore!
(*Sung*)
That's a swell way to lose a man.

You've found your perfect mate and it's been love from the
start.
He whispers, "You're the one to who I give my heart."

WONDERFUL TOWN

Don't say, "I love you too, my dear, let's never never part"—
(*Spoken*)
Just say, "I'm afraid you've made a grammatical error—it's
not 'To who I give my heart,' it's 'To *whom* I give my
heart'—You see, with the use of the preposition 'to,' 'who'
becomes the indirect object, making the use of 'whom'
imperative which I can easily show you by drawing a simple
chart"—
(*Waving good-bye toward an imaginary retreating
figure*)
That's a fine way to lose a man.

A fine fine fine fine way to lose a man,
A dandy way to lose a man—
Just be more well-informed than he,
You'll never hear "O Promise Me"—

Just show him where his grammar errs
Then mark your towels "hers" and "hers"—
Yes, girls, you too can lose your man
If you will use Ruth Sherwood's plan—
One hundred easy ways to lose a man!
(*She goes off as the lights dim.*)

ACT ONE

Scene IV

BAKER'S OFFICE *at the "Manhatter."*

AT RISE: BAKER *is seated behind desk.* RUTH *is seated in a chair opposite, talking fast.*

RUTH

—So you see, Mr. Baker, I worked on the Columbus *Globe* a couple of years—society page, sports, everything—and did a lot of writing on the side—but I'm afraid my stuff was a little too sophisticated for Columbus—so I took the big plunge and came to New York—

BAKER

(*Breaks in*)

Yes, I know—I did it myself but this is a mighty tough town —Maybe you should have come here gradually—by way of Cleveland first—

RUTH

Yes. They're awfully short of writers in Cleveland—

BAKER

Well, at least a few people in Ohio know you—

RUTH

That's why I left—

BAKER

(*Laughs*)

Look, Miss Sherwood, I'd like to help you, but I'm so

swamped now—If you just leave your stories here, somebody will read them.

RUTH
(*Puts envelope down*)
Are you sure? I get them back so fast that unless I take the subway, they beat me home!

BAKER
We read them, all right— (*He takes eyeglasses from breast pocket*) I had 20-20 vision when I left Duluth.

RUTH
Duluth? Maybe *you* should've come here gradually—and stopped at St. Paul—

BAKER
(*Grimly*)
Huh?

RUTH
—95 ways to go—

BAKER
What?

RUTH
Oh, dear—Mr. Baker, please—would you mind if I went out that door and came back in and started all over again?

BAKER
Forget it!

RUTH
And I was so anxious to make a good impression!

41

BAKER

Well, you made a strong one.
(ASSOCIATE EDITORS *enter with pile of manuscripts. They put them on* BAKER's *desk.*)

FIRST EDITOR (LINVILLE)

Light summer reading, Bob!

BAKER

Oh, no, not any more! (*To* RUTH)
See what I mean? Every one of those authors is convinced he's an undiscovered genius!

RUTH

(*Looks at pile of manuscripts, then up to* BOB)
Well, what do you advise me to do?

BAKER

(*From desk*)

Go home!
Go west!
Go back where you came from!
Oh, why did you ever leave Ohio?

RUTH

(*Rises*)

Because I think I have talent!

BAKER

A million kids just like you
Come to town every day

42

With stars in their eyes;
They're going to conquer the city,
They're going to grab off the Pulitzer Prize,
But it's a terrible pity
Because they're in for a bitter surprise.
And their stories all follow one line
>   (*Pointing with his arm to* FIRST EDITOR)

Like his,
>   (*Pointing to* SECOND EDITOR)

Like his,
>   (*To himself with both hands*)

Like mine.
>   (*To* RUTH)

Born in Duluth,
Natural writer,
Published at seven—genius type—
Wrote the school play,
Wrote the school paper—
Summa cum laude—all of that tripe—
Came to New York,
Got on the staff here—
This was my chance to be heard.
Well, since then I haven't written a word.

BAKER AND EDITORS
>   (*Strumming guitars—imaginary*)

What a waste,
What a waste,
What a waste of money and time!
>   (RUTH *turns and goes angrily as* BAKER *looks after her*
>   *sympathetically.*)

43

WONDERFUL TOWN

FIRST EDITOR

Man from Detroit—
Wonderful Artist—
Went to Picasso—Pablo said "Wow!"
Settled in France,
Bought him a beret,
Lived in Montmartre,
Really learned how,
Came to New York—had an exhibit,
Art critics made a big fuss,
Now he paints those tooth-paste ads on the bus!

EDITORS AND BAKER

What a waste,
What a waste,
What a waste of money and time!

SECOND EDITOR

Girl from Mobile,
Versatile actress—
Tragic or comic—
Any old play.
Suffered and starved,
Met Stanislavsky.
He said the world would
Cheer her some day.
Came to New York,
Repertoire ready,
Chekhov's and Shakespeare's and Wilde's—
Now they watch her flipping flapjacks at Childs'.

44

WONDERFUL TOWN

EDITORS AND BAKER

What a waste,
What a waste,
What a waste of money and time!

BAKER

Kid from Cape Cod,
Fisherman's family,
Marvelous singer—big baritone—
Rented his boat,
Paid for his lessons
Starved for his studies
Down to the bone—
Came to New York,
Aimed at the opera—
Sing "Rigoletto" his wish—
At the Fulton Market now he yells "Fish!"

EDITORS

What a waste,
What a waste,
What a waste of money and time!

BAKER
(*Looking off after* RUTH)
Go home! Go west!
Go back where you came from!
    (EDITORS *go.*)
Go home!
    (BAKER *goes to his desk, his mind still on* RUTH, *and picks*

45

up the envelope containing her manuscripts. He takes
them out and starts to read one.)

BAKER
(Reading)
"For Whom the Lion Roars"—by Ruth Sherwood.
"It was a fine day for a lion hunt. Yes, it was a good clean
day for an African lion hunt—a good clean day for a fine clean
kill."
> *(The lights go up on stage left as* BAKER *continues read-*
> *ing. In the ensuing* STORY VIGNETTES, *played stage left and*
> *musically underscored,* RUTH *portrays all the heroines.*
> *These are* RUTH's *ideas of sophisticated writing, and are*
> *acted in exaggerated satiric style.)*

BAKER
(Reading)
"Sandra Mallory stalked into the clearing with the elephant
gun."
> (SANDRA MALLORY [RUTH] *enters dazzlingly attired in a*
> *glamorous version of an African hunting outfit, a huge*
> *gun tucked casually under her arm.)*

BAKER
(Reading)
"Just behind Sandra was Harry Mallory, her husband, and
Randolph Rexford, the guide."
> *(They enter.* REXFORD *is an open-shirted, tight-lipped*
> *Gary Cooper type and* HARRY *is a small, ineffectual-look-*
> *ing man in an obvious state of terror, his gun shaking*
> *in his hands.)*

BAKER

(*Reading*)

"Nearby they could hear the fine clean roar of the lion."

(*There is a loud ominous lion roar.*)

REXFORD

(*Pointing out front*)

There he is, right in front of you, Mr. Mallory! (MALLORY *points his gun toward the oncoming roars, which become louder and louder as* REXFORD *continues*) No, not yet—wait until you see his eyes. That will be the fine, clean way to bag the Simba. No—not yet— Not yet, Mr. Mallory—

(MALLORY *dashes off, screaming*)

SANDRA

(*Flatly*)

My cigarette has gone out. (*She holds her cigarette up to her mouth. Contemptuously*) He ran—Harry, the brave hunter!

(*Her hand is trembling exaggeratedly.*)

REXFORD

(*Tensely*)

Your hand is trembling, Mrs. Mallory—

(*He grabs her hand, helping her light the cigarette.*)

SANDRA

(*Conscious of his grasp*)

It is nothing.

BAKER

(*Reading*)

"He gripped her hard. It was a clean fine grip. She remem-

47

bered Harry's grip. Like clean, fine oatmeal. Suddenly Sandra
Mallory felt the beat, beat, beat of Africa—"
(*Drums heard nearby.*)

SANDRA

(*Sexily to* REXFORD *as she undulates to the rhythm*)
Rexford—why do you hate me?

REXFORD

(*Tight-lipped*)
I have my job—Mrs. Mallory—and Mr. Mallory is your
husband.
(*There is a roar and terrified scream from off-stage.*)

SANDRA

(*Calmly*)
He *was* my husband. (*She drops her gun and walks toward
him passionately*) Rexford—

REXFORD

(*Moving toward her with equal passion*)
Mrs. Mallory—

SANDRA

(*Stepping nearer*)

Rexford—

REXFORD

(*Nearer—and now seething*)

Sandra—

SANDRA

(*Throwing her arms around him*)
Randolph!
(*He bends her backwards in a movie kiss.*)

BAKER

(*Incredulous*)

No!

(*There is a blackout on the African scene, as* BAKER *picks up the next manuscript a little more cautiously.*)

BAKER

(*Reading*)

"Twentieth-Century Blues." "It was squalid in that one room flat in Williamsburg without the windows, with the gray peeling plaster and the sound of rats scurrying inside the walls and the scratching phonograph across the hall screaming gee I'd like to see you lookin' swell baby diamond—" (BAKER *finally has to take a deep breath and plunge on*) "—bracelets Woolworth doesn't sell baby and Danny coming in gray and drawn like the gray plaster coming in clutching his guts with the gray rats inside his walls too yeah the gray rat pains of hunger yeah the twentieth-century hunger yeah—"

(DANNY *enters, a ragged proletarian figure in his undershirt, in the depths of despair and hunger. He is followed by* ESSIE [RUTH], *ludicrously ragged and obviously somewhat with child. They speak in the singsong Brooklynese used in the social-problem dramas of the '30's.*)

ESSIE

(*Dully*)

Danny—when we gonna get married?

DANNY

When—when—when—always naggin'—

49

ESSIE

They're talkin'—the neighbors are talkin'. Mamma looks at me funny like.

DANNY

It takes money, dream boat, to get married. The green stuff with the pictures of Lincoln—

ESSIE

Lincoln should see me now. Remember how swell life was gonna be— We was gonna have everything—a four-star trip to the moon—diamonds—yachts—shoes!

DANNY

Baby—

ESSIE

What's left, Danny—what's left?
(*They approach each other lumberingly with the same growing passion as in the first vignette.*)

DANNY
(*Stepping closer, arms open*)

Baby—

ESSIE

Danny—

DANNY

Baby—

ESSIE
(*Clutching him in an embrace*)

Danny!

BAKER

No!

(*There is a blackout on the vignette as he hurls the script down and very warily picks up the third.*)

"Exit Laughing"—"Everyone agreed that Tracy Farraday was marvelous. Everyone agreed that this was her greatest acting triumph. Everyone agreed that her breath-taking performance in 'Kiss Me, Herman' was the climax of a great career."
(*The lights go up on elegantly dressed party. Guests are discovered in a tableau.*)
"Everyone agreed that the plush opening night party at the Astor Hotel was a memorable occasion."
(*Everyone is indulging in upper-class merriment, with laughter and hysterical chitchat.* TRENT FARRADAY, *a stuffy society type, is kissing a girl as he holds her in a deep embrace.*)

WOMAN GUEST
(*Looking off*)

Here comes Tracy now!

ALL GUESTS

Tracy!
(TRACY *enters in superb evening clothes—the perfect picture of the glamorous actress. She takes a glamorous pose.*)

BAKER
(*Reading*)

"Everyone agreed that perhaps Tracy drank a bit too much."
(TRACY *suddenly staggers in cross-eyed, exaggerated drunkenness.*)

51

TRACY

(*Tallulah-ish*)

Has anyone seen that silly old husband of mine?

(TRACY *staggers to* TRENT—*taps him on shoulder. He is still deep in the embrace.*)

O, Trent—(TRENT *looks up from kiss*)—Have you got a match?

TRENT

Tracy—I'm leaving—I have found someone who needs me —appreciates me—

TRACY

You cahn't!

TRENT

(*Exiting with girl*)

You are not a woman, Tracy. You are a billboard.

TRACY

(*After him*)

No, no, Trent—I'll be different—I will— Don't go!

BAKER

(*Reading*)

"Everyone agreed that Tracy was a hypochondriac. Otherwise, why did she always carry a bottle of iodine?"

(TRACY, *throughout speech, is rummaging through her purse, pulls out red bottle of iodine and downs the contents.*)

TRACY

(*With bitter abandon, giving her greatest performance*)

Everybody! On with the party!

(*She executes a wild fandango—then suddenly clutching*

*her midriff in a paroxysm of agony, she crashes to the
floor.*)

MALE GUEST

Tracy!

WOMAN GUEST

Ah—she's just passing out!

TRACY

(*Pulling herself up on one elbow with difficulty—
gallant to the end*)

Yes! Everyone agrees—I'm just passing out—exit laughing!
Ha— Ha— Ha— Ha!

(*She laughs wildly and falls back dead, after a last con-
vulsive twitch.*)

GUESTS

(*Raising glasses in a toast to a noble lady, singing
in solemn chorale fashion*)

What a waste,

What a waste,

What a waste of money and time!

(BAKER *joins in the chorus—hurling his script down on
the desk. Blackout.*)

ACT ONE

Scene V

THE STREET. AT RISE: MRS. WADE *and* HELEN *come on.*

MRS. WADE

Whatever possessed you to move into a dreadful neighborhood like this, Helen? How do you ever expect to meet a nice young man down here?

HELEN

Oh, Mother, please! Let me live my own life!

MRS. WADE

(*Climbing steps—turning from top before going into house*) Life! You're just a child! You don't know what life is!

> (*Exits into house—*HELEN *following.* VALENTI *enters, followed by two* BOP GIRLS. FRANK LIPPENCOTT *enters. He carries a box of candy.*)

VALENTI

Skeet—skat—skattle-e-o-do— (*To girls*) Don't bother me, kids! Wait until you grow up!

> (*He's off, followed by kids.* EILEEN *comes on and sees* FRANK *peering in their window.*)

EILEEN

Oh, hello, Frank!

54

FRANK

Hello, Eileen! I just came down during my lunch hour. I've been thinking about you all morning.

EILEEN

You have?

FRANK

I brought you some chocolate-covered cherries we're running. We're featuring them all this week during our annual one-cent sale.

EILEEN
(*Taking candy from him*)

You're sweet.

FRANK

Well, I've got to get back to the drugstore. It's pandemonium down there.

EILEEN

Don't forget—we expect you for dinner tonight. I want you to meet my sister—she's in your neighborhood a lot.

FRANK

Oh—I'll be here all right.

EILEEN

Thanks for the chocolate-covered cherries.

FRANK

'Bye, Eileen—

EILEEN

'Bye, Frank!
(*She watches him go off and, starry-eyed, starts to sing*)

55

Mm— Mmm—
I'm a little bit in love.
Never felt this way before—
Mm— Mmm—
Just a little bit in love
Or perhaps a little bit more.

When he
Looks at me
Everything's hazy and all out of focus.
When he
Touches me
I'm in the spell of a strange hocus-pocus.
It's so
I don't know
I'm so
I don't know
I don't know—but I know
If it's love
Then it's lovely!

Mm— Mmm—
It's so nice to be alive
When you meet someone who bewitches you.
Will he be my all
Or did I just fall
A little bit
A little bit in love?

> (BOB BAKER *enters, goes to grill window and looks in.*
> EILEEN *pulls ribbon off candy box, goes to steps. She sees*
> BAKER *and stares coldly.*)

56

EILEEN

Well?

BAKER

(*Looking up from window*)

I was just looking for the young lady who lives in there—
my name's Baker—Robert Baker—

EILEEN

Did *Marty* send you?

BAKER

I beg your pardon.

EILEEN

I hate to ruin your afternoon, Mr. Baker, but Violet doesn't
live here any more.

BAKER

Violet?

EILEEN

You might tell Marty and all the boys. It'll save them a trip.

BAKER

I'm afraid you've got me confused with somebody else.

EILEEN

I have?

BAKER

Yes. I'm looking for Ruth Sherwood. She live here, doesn't
she?

EILEEN

Who—are you, Mr. Baker?

BAKER

I'm an associate editor of the *Manhatter*.

EILEEN

Oh, oh, I'm terribly sorry! Ruth'll be furious—I'm her sister, Eileen.

BAKER

How do you do, Miss Sherwood?

EILEEN

Ruth isn't in right now, but I'm sure she'll be right back. Won't you come in and wait?

BAKER

No, thanks. I'll drop by later.

EILEEN

You're sure, now?

BAKER

Oh, yes—

EILEEN

Because I know Ruth must be terribly anxious to see you—

BAKER

Well?

EILEEN

How about a nice, cool drink?

BAKER

Not now—thanks, Miss Sherwood—

58

EILEEN

Oh—*Eileen!*

BAKER

Eileen—

EILEEN

Mr. Baker—I mean, Robert—I have a wonderful idea! Why don't you come back and take pot luck with us?

BAKER

Well, I don't know—

EILEEN

Oh, please! I'm making a special dish tonight!

BAKER

Okay—what time?

EILEEN

Any time after seven!

BAKER

Swell, Eileen—see you later.

EILEEN

'Bye, Bob!
    (*She watches him go—and, with the same starry-eyed
    look as before, she sings*)
Mm— Mmm—
I'm a little bit in love
Never felt this way before
Mm— Mm—(*music continues*)
    (LONIGAN *enters slowly*)
O hello, Officer!

59

LONIGAN
(*Suspiciously*)

Yeah.

(THE WRECK *enters and goes to house. He is carrying a rolled-up Army mattress.*)

WRECK

I borrowed a mattress, Eileen. That floor in your place is awful hard!

(WRECK *disappears into house.* LONIGAN *looks warily to* EILEEN, *who turns, startled, and puts a hand to her mouth. Blackout.*)

ACT ONE

Scene VI

THE BACK YARD. *This is the "garden" that* APPOPOLOUS *boasts about. It's a dismal place, sunk deep among the tenements that surround it. There are a moldy tree, a couple of chairs and a bench. Across from the girls' kitchen we see the back entrance of* NINO's, *an Italian restaurant.* AT RISE: WRECK *is at an ironing board, pressing some of the girls' things.*

WRECK

"I'm a rambling Wreck—
From Trenton Tech—
And a helluva engineer—"
    (WAITER *comes out of* NINO's *and is joined by Italian* CHEF.)

CHEF

E arrivato la padrone— E meglio cominciare a lavorare.

WAITER

Peccato. Si sta cosi bene qui fuore.

CHEF

Be. Cosi e la vita.
    (RUTH *comes in from kitchen.*)

RUTH

Any mail?

WRECK

Yeah, one of your stories came back.

RUTH

From the *Manhatter*?

WRECK

No, *Collier's*. (RUTH *picks up manuscript in envelope at window sill, changing address with a pencil.*)
Hot, ain't it?

RUTH

Yah. I feel as if I'm living in my own little world, mailing these to myself.

WRECK

Hey, which way do you want these pleats turned?

RUTH

(*Glances at him wearily*)

Toward Mecca.

(*The phone rings.* WRECK *goes to window sill and answers it.*)

WRECK

The Sherwood residence—who do you want?—Eleanor? You mean Eileen—She's not in. (*Annoyed*) This is the butler—Who the hell are *you*?

RUTH

(*Grabbing phone*)

Wreck! Hello? . . . Who is this, please? . . . Chick Clark? Oh, yes, Mr. Clark. This is her sister—Ruth. . . . No, she's not in right now . . . any minute . . . I'll tell her. . . . 'Bye.

(*Hangs up. Makes note on pad at window sill.*)

WRECK

That Eileen does all right for herself. And the funny part of it is, she's a good girl.

RUTH
(*Eyeing him*)
When did you find *that* out?

WRECK

No, you sense those things. I never made a pass at you, but I could swear *you're* all right.

RUTH

That's the story of my life.
(*She goes off with manuscript as* HELEN *enters.*)

WRECK

Hy'ah, Sugar Foot!

HELEN

Hi.

WRECK

Do you miss me, honey?

HELEN

Of course I miss you. Now *I* have to do all the housework. (*Looking at laundry*) Huh! You never ironed that good for me!

WRECK

Now look, honey—!
(MRS. WADE *appears in street above them.* HELEN *ducks behind ironing board, her rear facing the audience.*)

63

MRS. WADE
(*Staring at* WRECK)

Well, I never!

WRECK

What are *you* lookin' at, you old bat?

MRS. WADE

How dare you!
(*She goes off indignantly.*)

WRECK
(*Shouts after her*)

Didn't you ever see a man in shorts before?

HELEN
(*Wails*)

Wreck! That was Mom!

WRECK

You mean that old wagon was your mother?

HELEN

You've got to get out of here!

WRECK

Where am I gonna sleep?

HELEN

If we could scrape up a few dollars you could stay at the
"Y" till Mother leaves.

WRECK

We're tryin' to dig up a coupla bucks and your mother's got
a mattressful!

HELEN

If only we had somethin' left to hock.

WRECK

Hey—wait a minute! (*Goes to kitchen*) If anyone comes,
whistle "Dixie."
   (*There is a blast from the subway.* HELEN *jumps as*
   WRECK *reappears with* APPOPOLOUS' *"blue-green" canvas.*)

HELEN

That's one of Appopolous'. They won't lend you a dime
on it!

WRECK

This fancy frame might be good for a coupla bucks. Take
it over to Benny's and see what you can get on it!
   (HELEN *exits with picture.* DELIVERY KID *enters from
   street with basket of vegetables.*)

KID
(*Adoringly*)
Hey, Wreck—getting ready for the football season?

WRECK

Oh, I keep in shape!

KID
(*Centering the "ball"—a head of cabbage*)
Hey—signals?

65

WRECK

45—26—7—hip!
(WRECK *catches ball.*)

CHEF
(*Enters in front of* NINO'S—*to* KID)
E tu che diavalo fai con quel cavalo?

KID
(*To* WRECK)
Pass.
(WRECK *passes to* KID—*who passes to* WAITER, *who catches cabbage in his stomach.*)

CHEF
Che pazzerela!
(*Waving an angry hand at* KID, *who passes him basket with vegetables.* CHEF *exits.*)

KID
Well, you certainly look in good shape for the football season.

WRECK
Yeah—for all the good it does me!
(*Goes wearily back to ironing and sings*)
Look at me now
Four years of college
Famous professors
Tutoring me
Scholarship kid

66

WONDERFUL TOWN

Everything paid for
Food and vacations
All of it free
Day that I left
Everyone gathered
Their cheering still rings in my ears—
 (*Carried away by memories, he executes some of the old
 cheers with great vigor*)
Ray Wreck rah
Rah Wreck ray
Rah Wreck
Wreck rah
Rah Wreck Wreck
W-e-c, R-e-k, R-e-q
Wreck, we love you!
 (*Singing bravura*)
'Cause I could pass a football
Like nothin' you have ever seen!
 (*A crowd has gathered on the street, watching him.
 They cheer*)
Couldn't spell a lick
Couldn't do arithmetic
One and one made three
Thought that dog was c-a-t
But I could pass a football
Like nothing you have ever seen

Couldn't write my name
Couldn't translate "je vous aime"
Never learned to read
Mother Goose or André Gide

WONDERFUL TOWN

But I could pass a football
Like nothing you have ever seen

Couldn't figure riddles
Puzzles made me pout
Where the hell was Moses when the lights went out?
I couldn't even tell red from green
Get those verbs through my bean
But I was buddies with the Dean
Like nothing you have ever seen

Passed without a fuss
English Lit and Calculus
Never had to cram
Even passed the bar exam
Because I passed that football
Like nothing you have ever seen

Then there was the week
Albert Einstein came to speak
Relativity
Guess who introduced him? Me!
'Cause I could pass a football
Like nothing you have ever seen

Had no table manners
Used ta dunk my roll
Always drunk the water from the fingerbowl
Though I would not get up for any she
The Prexy's mom—age ninety-three

Got up and gave her seat to me
Like nothing you did ever see

In our Hall of Fame
There's a statue with my name
There we stand, by heck
Lincoln, Washington and Wreck
'Cause I could pass that football
Like nothing you have ever seen!
>   (WRECK *and* CROWD *of assorted* VILLAGERS *do a "football"*
>   *dance, with* WRECK *ending up with a pile of players, hope-*
>   *lessly outclassed. He sticks his head out from under,*
>   *weakly.)*
'Cause I could pass that football!
Like nothing you have ever—ever seen!
>   (CROWD *pulls away.* WRECK *staggers and collapses in their*
>   *arms. At the end of number, the* CROWD *goes off.* HELEN
>   *enters with pawn ticket.)*

HELEN
Two bucks—here's the ticket.

EILEEN
(*Enters from studio*)
Gee, Wreck—the laundry looks swell.

HELEN
(*Coldly*)
Too bad he's leaving, isn't it?

EILEEN

Oh, is he?

HELEN

Yes, and it's about time, too.
(RUTH *enters from alley.*)

WRECK

Stop racin' your motor! I told her there was nothing to it!

RUTH

Nothing to *what?*

EILEEN

Ruth, do you know what she had the nerve to insinuate?

RUTH

Was it something with sex in it?

WRECK

Why, if I thought about Eileen in that way— May God strike
me dead on this spot!
(*He raises his hand solemnly and there's a tremendous
Boom! from below. He shrinks guiltily.*)

RUTH

(*Looking up*)
He's everywhere all right.

HELEN

Come on, Wreck!
(*They go off.* VIOLET *enters from house.*)

70

VIOLET
(*Cheerfully*)

Hello, girls.

RUTH
(*Stares*)

Hello.

VIOLET

I'm Violet. I used to live in this fleabag before you girls got it.

EILEEN

Oh, so *you're* Violet.

VIOLET

Say, have I had any callers the last coupla weeks—since you kids moved in?

RUTH
(*Grimly*)

One or two.

VIOLET

I thought so. A lot of my friends don't know I moved yet. In case they come around—would you mind giving out my new cards? (*She takes thick pack of calling cards from purse and hands them to* EILEEN.) Thanks loads. So long.
(*She goes.*)

RUTH

The spiritual type.
(EILEEN *carries cards to window sill.*)

EILEEN
(*Looking at note pad*)
Oh, did Chick Clark call?

RUTH

Yes. Who's he?

EILEEN

He's a newspaperman. I met him in an elevator. We got to talking and I told him about you. He seemed very interested in you.

RUTH

So interested in me, I'll bet he can't wait to get you alone.

EILEEN

What've we got for dinner, Ruth?

RUTH

What do you think? Spaghetti and meat balls.

EILEEN

Haven't we polished that off yet? We've had it all week!

RUTH
(*Flatly*)

It closes tonight.

EILEEN

Well, we simply can't give that to Bob.

RUTH

Bob? I can't keep up with you. Who's *Bob*?

EILEEN

You know, Bob Baker, from the *Manhatter*. Don't play dumb!

72

RUTH

Mr. Baker! No! (*Turns* EILEEN *around*) Where did you meet him?

EILEEN

He dropped by to see you, and naturally I asked him to dinner.

RUTH

Naturally! (*Grabs* EILEEN, *kisses her*) Oh, darling! You are terrific! I'd never have the nerve!

EILEEN

Well, for goodness sake, why not? He's just a *boy*—

RUTH

(*Looks around helplessly*)

How can we fix this dump up a little? (*Closing kitchen door*) Eileen, promise me you won't take him in there!

EILEEN

Of course not. We'll eat in the garden—al fresco.

RUTH

Ah—

EILEEN

Oh, dear—I just remembered. I asked Frank over tonight.

RUTH

Who?

EILEEN

You know—Walgreen's—

RUTH

Oh, no! How can you mix a soda jerk with an editor?

EILEEN

He's *not* a jerk! He's the manager!

RUTH

Okay—okay— Gee, if a man like Mr. Baker comes to see me personally, he must really be interested!

EILEEN

Of course he's interested.

RUTH

And we can't even offer him a cocktail.

EILEEN

We could tell him it's too hot to drink.

RUTH
(*Nods*)
But cold enough for spaghetti.

EILEEN

Hmmm—smell that chicken cacciatori at Nino's. Maybe I ought to have a little talk with Mr. Nino.

RUTH

Do you know him too?

EILEEN

No, but I will—he's our neighbor, isn't he?

74

(*She goes into* NINO'S. CHICK CLARK *enters from street above.*)

CHICK

Hello. (*Coming down stairs, consulting matchbook*) I'm lookin' for a party named Sherwood—Eleanor Sherwood.

RUTH

You mean Eileen. You must be Mr. Clark?

CHICK

Yeah. Who are you?

RUTH

I'm her sister.

CHICK
(*Doubtfully*)
Her sister? She's a blonde, *good-looking* kid, ain't she?

RUTH
(*Grimly*)
Yes, she's a blonde, good-looking kid.

CHICK
(*Loosening his collar*)
Wow, it's absolute murder down here, ain't it? (*Staring overhead*) What is this—an abandoned mine shaft?

RUTH

Are you planning to be with us long, Mr. Clark?

CHICK

Eileen asked me to take pot luck with her.

75

FRANK

(Off stage)

Hello? Anyone home? (FRANK *appears at window in studio*)
Oh, hello, the front door was open. Is Eileen home?

RUTH

You're Mr. Lippencott, aren't you? Come in.
(She motions to steps. Door opens. LIPPENCOTT *appears, carrying bottle of red wine. Trips down stairs. Recovers himself. Pulls out comb and combs hair.)*

FRANK

Gee, I'm sorry. I didn't know there was any—
(Shakes hands with RUTH.)

RUTH

Oh, that's all right. Everybody does that.

FRANK

I guess you're Eileen's sister. I can see a family resemblance, all right.

RUTH

Why, I'm very flattered.

FRANK

Of course, you're a different type.

RUTH

Yes, I see what you mean. Eileen'll be back in a minute—
(Glancing to café) She's just fixing dinner. *(Looking at* CHICK)
Oh, I want you to meet Mr. Clark—

76

(FRANK *goes to* CHICK, *to shake hands.* CHICK *ignores his hand.*)

CHICK

There ain't too much oxygen down here as it is.

RUTH

Mr. Lippencott is with Walgreen's.

CHICK

Yeah? I buy all my clothes there.

FRANK

No, it's a drugstore.

CHICK
(*Groans and looks at bottle with interest*)
What's in the bottle?

FRANK
(*To* CHICK *coldly*)
A very fine California Burgundy-type wine. (*To* RUTH) I thought it would go good with the spaghetti. (*Hands her wine*) It's a special we're running this week.

RUTH
(*Looking at bottle sadly*)
So's our spaghetti.

FRANK

Huh?

RUTH

Has this heat affected your business?

77

FRANK

Why, we pray for heat waves.

CHICK

Oh, you *do,* eh?

FRANK

Our fountain turnover is double. I'm lucky to get away at all.

RUTH

Oh, *we're* the lucky ones.

EILEEN

(*Entering, to* FRANK)

Oh, Frank, I'm terribly sorry I wasn't here to greet you! (*To* RUTH) Ruth, what do you think?

RUTH

What?

EILEEN

Mr. Nino's in Italy. He won't be back till Labor Day. (*To* CHICK, *in dismay*) Oh, hello, Mr. Clark!

CHICK

Hy'ah, gorgeous!

EILEEN

Oh, Ruth, this is that newspaper gentleman I was telling you about who was so interested in you.

CHICK

That's right. I gave the city editor a big pitch already—

78

(*Lasciviously*) You won't believe this, baby, but I've been turnin' you over in my mind all afternoon.

(EILEEN *laughs uneasily as* RUTH *nods.*)

Gee, this is great. I always wanted to live in the Village in a place like this.

RUTH

What stopped you?

FRANK

Well, in my position in the drugstore you've got to keep up appearances.

RUTH

I see. Where the Liggetts speak only to the Walgreens and the Walgreens speak only to God.

(CHICK *grabs* EILEEN's *hand. She pulls away.*)

EILEEN

I'd better set the table. (*Goes to kitchen*) Where shall we dine—inside or outside?

CHICK

Which is *this*?

(BOB BAKER *appears from street, waving envelope with manuscript.*)

BAKER

Hello!

EILEEN

Oh, hello, Bob!

RUTH

Hello, Mr. Baker! Sorry I wasn't in when you called.

79

BAKER

That's all right—

RUTH

I'd like you to meet Mr. Clark—Mr. Lippencott— This is Mr. Baker—

FRANK

Pleased to meet you.
(*Holds out his hand, which* BAKER *shakes.*)

CHICK

What the hell is this, a block party?

RUTH

You're quite a card, aren't you, Mr. Clark? (*Puts wine on window sill*) Mr. Lippencott brought you some wine, dear.

EILEEN

Oh, how sweet! Shall we sit down?
(*She motions the others to join her and there is a general embarrassed shuffling about for chairs. She pulls* BOB *down beside her on her chair.* CHICK *brings a chair forward and* RUTH, *assuming it is for her, goes toward it, but* CHICK *sits on it himself. She gets her own and the five wind up in a tight uncomfortable group facing one another with nothing to say.* EILEEN *after a pause*)
Well—here we are—all together—
(*There is a dry discordant vamp in the orchestra expressing the atmosphere of embarrassed silence, which is repeated during every pause in the following song and conversation. It seems to grow more mocking and desperate at each repetition. After another pause they all*

start speaking at once very animatedly and then dwindle
off. Pause again. EILEEN *giggles nervously. Pause.*)

FRANK
(*Starting bravely*)
At the bottom of the vanilla—
(*He has a terrific coughing fit.* BAKER *slaps his back, and*
he sits down—and combs his hair.)
It's nothing.
(*Vamp.*)

EILEEN
(*Singing, over-brightly, after a pause*)
Mmmm—mmmm—it's so nice to sit around—
And chat—
Nice people, nice talk,
A balmy summer night,
A bottle of wine—
Nice talk—nice people,
Nice feeling—nice talk—
The combination's right
And everything's fine—

Nice talk—nice people
It's friendly—it's gay
To sit around this way.
What more do you need?
Just talk—and people.
For that can suffice
When both the talk and people are so nice—
(*She finishes lamely as the vamp is played again. Pause.*)

FRANK

(*Settling back in chair with a hollow, unconvincing laugh*)
Ha ha—Funny thing happened at the counter today—Man
comes in—Sort of tall like—Nice looking refined type—Red
bow tie—and all. Well sir, he orders a banana split—That's
our jumbo special—twenty-eight cents—Three scoops—chocolate, strawberry, vanilla—choice of cherry or caramel sauce—
chopped nuts—whipped cream—Well, sir, he eats the whole
thing—I look at his plate and I'll be hornswoggled if he doesn't
leave the whole banana—doesn't touch it—not a bite—Don't
you see?—If he doesn't like bananas, what does he order a
banana split for?—He coulda had a sundae—nineteen cents—
Three scoops—Chocolate—Strawberry—Vanilla—
(*He dwindles off as vamp is played again.*)

RUTH

(*Making a noble attempt to save the day*)
I was re-reading *Moby Dick* the other day and— Oh, I haven't
read it since—I'm sure none of us has— It's worth picking up
again— It's about this whale—
(*Her futile attempt hangs heavy on the air. Vamp again.*)

CHICK

(*Even he is driven by desperation to attempt sociability*)
Boy, it's hot! Reminds me of that time in Panama—I was
down there on a story—I was in this, well, dive— And there
was this broad there—What was her name?— Marquita?—
Maroota? (*Warming to his subject*) Ahh, what's the difference what her name was—That dame was built like a brick—
(*A sharp drum crash cuts him off and the vamp is played
with hysterical speed and violence. The four others spring*

to their feet horrified and, as CHICK *stands by puzzled,*
they cover up with a sudden outburst of animated talk
and laughter expressed by a rapid rendition of "Nice
People, Nice Talk" with EILEEN *singing an insane colo-*
ratura obbligato as the music builds to a thunderous
close.)

ALL

Nice people, nice talk,
A balmy summer night,
A bottle of wine—
Nice talk, nice people,
Nice feeling—nice talk.
The combination's right
And everything's fine.

Nice talk, nice people—
It's friendly, it's gay
To sit around this way.
What more do you need?
Just talk and people.
For that can suffice
When both the talk and people are so nice
It's nice!
     (*A closing orchestra chord.*)

RUTH
(*Gets bottle*)
Let's have a drink, shall we?

EILEEN
(*To* FRANK)
Do we need ice?

FRANK

No, this wine should be served at the temperature of the room.

CHICK

Then you'd better cook it a coupla hours.

APPOPOLOUS

(*Entering from stairs*)

Congratulate me, young ladies!

Today is the big day! I'm entering my painting in the WPA Art Contest!

(*He goes into studio.*)

BAKER

Ruth, who's that?

RUTH

Our landlord—Rasputin.

APPOPOLOUS

(*Comes back, heavily*)

What kind of a funny game is going on here? Where is it? Who took it?

RUTH

What?

APPOPOLOUS

You know everybody who goes into your apartment.

RUTH

We don't know *half* of them.

84

APPOPOLOUS

Please, I know you girls are hard up. Tell me what you did
with it and there'll be no questions asked.

EILEEN

You don't think we stole it?

APPOPOLOUS

If you didn't—who did?

RUTH

Maybe it was the same gang that swiped the Mona Lisa.

APPOPOLOUS
(*Goes angrily*)

You won't be so humorous when I come back with a cop!

RUTH
(*To* BAKER *anxiously*)

I hope you don't take any of that seriously, Mr. Baker.

BAKER

Of course not.

FRANK
(*Scared*)

Do you think he's really going to call the police?

EILEEN

The police won't pay any attention to him—he's always
calling them!

85

CHICK

Well, let's crack that bottle before the wagon gets here!

EILEEN

I'll open it and get some glasses. Do you want to help me, Frank?

CHICK

(*Stepping in*)

I'll help ya, Eleanor—(*Turning to* FRANK) You stay out here and hand them a few laughs.

(EILEEN *starts in to house.* CHICK *follows.*)

FRANK

Oh, is that so?

(*Trips up steps into house.*)

RUTH

(*To* BAKER, *sadly*)

If you'd like to make your getaway now, Mr. Baker, I'll understand.

BAKER

No, I'm enjoying it.

RUTH

Did you get a chance to read those stories?

BAKER

I certainly did!

(WRECK *and* HELEN *appear in street.*)

RUTH

Well, what did you think?

86

WRECK
(*Coming down stairs*)
Oh, I'm sorry, Ruth—didn't know you had company.

HELEN
(*With him*)
Can we come in?

RUTH
(*Groans*)
Yes, please do. (*To kitchen*) Two more glasses, Eileen!

WRECK
I talked it over with Helen, and she wants to apologize.

RUTH
(*Quickly*)
That's not necessary—Mr. Baker—This is Mr. Loomis—and his intended. (*They shake hands.* BAKER *eyes his shorts anxiously*) Mr. Loomis is in training.

BAKER
Oh.
(FRANK *enters from studio with tray and glasses of wine.*)

FRANK
(*From top of steps*)
This wine was—(*Stepping carefully down*) made by a Frenchman in California.
(EILEEN *comes through studio door, carrying two more glasses.*)

EILEEN

Oh, hello there—(*She hands glass to* RUTH. CHICK *follows through studio door, carrying his own glass.* FRANK *passes tray to* WRECK *and* HELEN *and moves upstage with tray*) What a magnificent bouquet!

RUTH

Drink up, everyone—it's later than you think! Here's to us and Burgundy, California!
> (*They all have raised glasses in toast. There's a "boom" from below.* FRANK *jumps and spills his wine all over his new white suit.*)

FRANK

Gee, what was that?

EILEEN
> (*Stares at the wine stain miserably*)

Oh, Frank, I'm terribly sorry!

FRANK
> (*Looking down at his suit pathetically*)

What—what happened?

RUTH

The new subway—
> (*Wipes off wine.*)

FRANK
> (*Wails*)

Does red wine stain?

88

EILEEN

Not if you rub salt on it.
(*Wipes off wine.*)

CHICK

You better get a bagful!

FRANK

I just got this suit. It's brand new!

CHICK

Ah, you can't even notice it!
(*He starts to laugh. They all join in, hysterically.* FRANK
stands in the center, stricken. HELEN *sinks to the floor
in her laughter.*)

FRANK
(*Backing to stairs, he starts up them*)
Well, if you think it's so funny, I'll go!

EILEEN
(*Starts to follow*)
Frank—don't go! Wait! (*Turning to the others*) Oh, dear
—he's really angry.

MRS. WADE
(*Off stage*)
Helen, are you in there?

HELEN

Yes, Mother.

89

RUTH

Won't you come in, Mrs. Wade?

MRS. WADE

(*Entering*)

Most certainly not. Helen, I want you to come out of there immediately!

HELEN

But, Mother.

MRS. WADE

I will not have you associating with those depraved women and their consort!

RUTH AND EILEEN

What?

WRECK

Who's a consort?

HELEN

Please, Mother—

MRS. WADE

Not another word. You come right along with me. Don't you dare talk to my Helen again. You're not fit to associate with decent people!

(*She pushes* HELEN *out.*)

WRECK

I'm gonna wait till Mother's Day—(*Making fist*) and sock her!

(*He goes.*)

EILEEN

Bob, I don't know what you must think of us, but really, it isn't so.

BAKER
(*Grins*)

I'm sure it isn't.

RUTH

Well, you must admit—for a place with a bad location and no neon sign, we're doing a hell of a business.

EILEEN
(*Brightly*)

Dinner, anyone?

BAKER

Fine!

EILEEN
(*Going to kitchen*)

I'd better heat the entrée.

CHICK
(*Following close behind*)

We'll warm it up together, Eleanor!
(*They go off.*)

RUTH

Funny, I'm not a bit hungry.

BAKER

I'm starving. And I smell something delicious!

RUTH
(*Looks at* NINO's)

Trade Winds.

EILEEN'S VOICE

Mr. Clark, please! Not while I'm trying to cook!

BAKER

While we have a minute, before anything else happens, I'd like to talk to you about your stories—

RUTH

Oh, do, please! You mean you actually read them yourself?

BAKER

I certainly did—You have a lot of talent, Miss Sherwood—

RUTH

Do you really think so?

BAKER

Yes, I do—(RUTH *turns away, tearfully*) What's the matter?

RUTH

Nothing—

BAKER

You're crying—

RUTH

(*Turning back to him*)
It's just an allergy I have to good news—

BAKER

You really should have more faith in yourself—

RUTH

Thanks, I'm beginning to—

92

BAKER

And once you get on the right track, you're going to do some good work.

RUTH

Right track?

BAKER

Look Ruth. Have you ever gone on a safari in the African veldt?

RUTH

No.

BAKER

And have you ever lived in a cold-water tenement?

RUTH

No.

BAKER

Then why do you write that stuff? Write about something you know—something you've actually experienced.

RUTH

I write the things I feel! I put myself in every one of those characters!

BAKER

Then you must be hopelessly repressed.

RUTH

That's a terrible thing to say! I'm the most normal person you'll ever meet!

BAKER

That's a sure sign. All inhibited people think they're normal.

RUTH

Oh! So now I'm inhibited!

BAKER

(*Turns to her*)

I'm afraid so—if you claim you're really those frustrated heroines.

RUTH

Repressed! Inhibited! Frustrated! What *else* am I?

BAKER

Don't take it personally—

RUTH

How else can I take it?

BAKER

I'm just trying to help you—

RUTH

What are you, an editor or a psychoanalyst?

BAKER

I should've known better—You can't take it—You'll never get anywhere till you learn humility—

RUTH

When did you learn yours?

(*Runs into studio quickly.* BAKER *watches her.*)

WONDERFUL TOWN

BAKER

(With weary anger)

All right! Good-bye!
You've taught me my lesson!
Get mixed up with a genius from Ohio!
It happens over and over—
I pick the sharp intellectual kind.
Why couldn't this time be different,
Why couldn't she—only be
Another kind— A different kind of girl
  (As the lights dim, he pictures the kind of relationship
  he would like to have, but has never known.)
I love a quiet girl,
I love a gentle girl
Warm as sunlight,
Soft, soft as snow.

Her smile, a tender smile,
Her voice, a velvet voice,
Sweet as music,
Soft, soft as snow.

When she is near me
The world's in repose.
We need no words
She sees— She knows.

But where is my quiet girl,
Where is my gentle girl,
Where is the special girl,
Who is soft, soft as snow?

Somewhere—
Somewhere—
My quiet girl.

> (*As he walks slowly off,* RUTH *enters from the kitchen
> and watches him go, with the hopeless feeling of having
> lost him.*)

RUTH
(*Sings*)

I know a quiet girl,
Hoping—waiting—
But he'll never know.

> (*The music continues. There is a crash of dishes from
> the kitchen.* RUTH *turns suddenly—looks toward kitchen
> —her reverie broken.*)

EILEEN
(*Off stage*)

Now look what you made me do! (*Entering from studio,*
CHICK *follows*) The spaghetti—it's all over the kitchen floor!
Really, Mr. Clark!

CHICK

You're so darn jumpy—! (*Goes to stairs*) Okay, I'll run down
to the corner and get some sandwiches and beer! Be right back!

> (*He's off.*)

EILEEN

Where's Bob?

RUTH

Gone.

EILEEN

Isn't he coming back?

96

RUTH

If he does, he's crazy after the way I treated him.

EILEEN

Gee, Ruth, what happened?

RUTH

I'd rather not discuss it—I'm too frustrated. (*There's a "boom" from below. She looks down wearily*) Go on! Blow us up and get it over with!

EILEEN

Gee, Ruth, if you start to feel that way, who's going to hold me up?

RUTH

Oh, I'm not worried about you—not while there's a man alive.

EILEEN

After all, men are only an escape.
(*The phone rings.* EILEEN *hurries to it.*)

RUTH

Comes another escape—

EILEEN

(*On phone*)
Sherwood residence—Miss *Ruth* Sherwood?

RUTH

For *me?*

EILEEN

Who's calling please?—What? Wait a minute— Just a second! (*To* RUTH) Ruth, it's Chick Clark's paper. Mr. Bains of the city room wants to talk to you—

(EILEEN *hands phone to* RUTH.)

RUTH

Hello?—Yes—yes, Mr. Bains. This is she—*her*—*she*. Thank you, Mr. Bains. That's wonderful! Yes, yes, of course. (*To* EILEEN) Paper and pencil quick. Take this down!

(EILEEN *reaches over for pad and pencil from window*.)

EILEEN

What is it? What happened?

RUTH

Yes, Mr. Bains—I'm ready! Sands—Street—Brooklyn—I understand—Yes, right away, Mr. Bains! Thank you—thank you very much. (*She hangs up, looks up excitedly*) I can't believe it!

EILEEN

What did he say? What did he want?

RUTH

He's giving me a chance to show what I can do—an assignment over in Brooklyn!

EILEEN

Brooklyn? What happened there?

RUTH

A Brazilian training ship just came in—like Annapolis—
only these fellows are all young coffee millionaires. I'm going
aboard to get a human-interest story.

EILEEN

Coffee millionaires! Well, you're not going over there with
a run in your stocking! Take it off!
 (*They sit on bench. Both remove stockings, exchange
 them. Conversation continues throughout.*)

RUTH

What a break! Isn't it wonderful! I'll show him!

EILEEN

Who?

RUTH

Never mind! Inhibited, huh?

EILEEN

What?

RUTH

I'll get a job on my own! Who does he think he is? (*Fin-
ished with stocking, she jumps up*) Have you got any money?

EILEEN

Who—*me?*

RUTH

How am I going to get over there?

EILEEN

The milk bottles!
(RUTH *picks up bottles near door, grabs her hat and rushes to stairs.*)

RUTH
(*Climbing stairs*)

Wish me luck!
(EILEEN *follows.*)

EILEEN

Good luck!
(RUTH *exits noisily, milk bottles clanging.* EILEEN *turns back, picks up tray with wine glasses, exits into studio.* WAITER *enters with gallon glass jug of cheap wine.* CHEF *enters with two Chianti bottles in straw and funnel.*)

CHEF

Il vino?

WAITER

Porta qui le bottiglie. Eco!
(*Pulls two straw bottles from behind back.* WAITER *pours from cheap bottle into straw one. When first bottle is full,* CHEF *takes funnel and puts it into second bottle.*)

CHICK
(*Entering from street carrying package from grocery store.*
EILEEN *comes out of studio*)

Dinner for two—comin' right up!

EILEEN
(*Takes sandwiches*)

Oh, how nice!

CHICK

Let's go in the kitchen. It's stiflin' out here!
(CHEF *and* WAITER *go off with bottles.*)

EILEEN

(*Going to bench*)
Oh, this is much pleasanter! (CHICK *sits next to her and
makes a pass at her shoulder which she shrugs off. She puts
bag with food between them*) It was awfully sweet of you to
get Ruth a chance.
(*Opening wrapper, pulling out sandwich.*)

CHICK

A pleasure! (*He pats her hand and puts arm around her.
She hands him sandwich in hand which has been groping
around her back. He puts sandwich on bench, his arms around
her again*)—And the next thing, we're gonna get your career
straightened out.

EILEEN

(*Struggling, rises*)
Please! You'll have to excuse me, Mr. Clark!

CHICK

Excuse ya! After all the trouble I went to get rid of that
eagle-eyed sister of yours.

EILEEN

(*Staring*)
What? That call Ruth got was from the editor, wasn't it?

CHICK

What are you worryin' about? I'm handling it—

EILEEN

It was *you*! You sent Ruth on a wild goose chase!

CHICK
(*Shrugs*)
I'll give her a coupla bucks for her trouble.

EILEEN

She was so excited. How am I ever going to tell her? You
get out of here!

CHICK

Now that's a lousy attitude to take! (*Phone rings*) Let it
ring!

EILEEN

Hello? Oh, Mr. Baker—hello, Bob!

CHICK
(*Into phone*)

Call back later!

EILEEN
(*To* CHICK)

How dare you! (*Into phone*) Oh, just somebody who's
leaving—(*To* CHICK) Now stop this nonsense! (EILEEN, *into
phone*)—Ruth? No, she's gone to Brooklyn—(*To* CHICK—
hand over phone) Skunk! (*Into phone, elegantly*) Oh, you
don't have to apologize—we never got to dinner anyway. Me?
I guess I'll wait for Ruth—I always feel silly eating alone—

CHICK

Alone! How about me and them baloney sandwiches!

EILEEN

(*Into phone*)

Why, Bob, how nice! I'd love to have dinner with you—
(*Glaring at* CHICK) Yes, I'll be waiting—
(*Hangs up. Picks sandwich from window sill.*)

CHICK

That's the worst double-cross I ever got! A fine little sneak
you turned out to be! (EILEEN *starts to eat sandwich.* CHICK
grabs it from her hand, as she is taking a bite. CHICK *goes to
bench, picks up empty bag, stuffs* EILEEN'S *sandwich into it*)
I ain't fattenin' you up for someone else!
(*Blackout.*)

ACT ONE

Scene VII

THE NAVY YARD. AT RISE: SHORE PATROLMAN *doing sentry duty.* RUTH *enters, passing* SHORE PATROLMAN.

SHORE PATROLMAN

Just a minute, Miss! Where's your pass?

RUTH

Oh, it's all right—Press—I'm a reporter—

SHORE PATROLMAN

You gotta have a pass.

RUTH

I just want to interview those Brazilian cadets.

SHORE PATROLMAN

Look—I'm tryin' to tell you—a pass—

RUTH

Well, where can I get one?

SHORE PATROLMAN

You can't— Commandant's office is closed. Tomorrow.

RUTH

Oh, please—my job depends on it!

104

SHORE PATROLMAN

So does mine.

(BRAZILIAN CADET *enters.*)

FIRST CADET

(*Eying* RUTH *with some interest. After all, she's a woman*)
Hello.

RUTH

(*To* SHORE PATROLMAN)

Is that one of them? (SHORE PATROLMAN *nods. She steps to*
CADET), Excuse me, Admiral. I'm from the press, and I'd like to
ask you a few questions—

(CADET *shrugs his shoulders, blankly.*)

SHORE PATROLMAN

That means he don't understand.

RUTH

Thanks. I know that much Portuguese myself.

(*Seven more* CADETS *enter, enveloping* RUTH *in their
midst, and talking loudly.*)

Ah! Any of you Admirals speak English?

SECOND CADET

Si! English!

RUTH

What do you think of America?

SECOND CADET

American dance—Conga!

105

RUTH

No, no! Conga's a Brazilian dance!

FIRST CADET

No—Cubano!

SECOND CADET

Conga *American* dance! You show Conga!

RUTH

Then will you tell me?

ALL

Si! Si!

RUTH

It's like this. One, two, three, kick. One, two, three, kick.
(*She shuffles from side to side in Conga step. They follow clumsily. She ad libs: That's fine! You've got it! That's right! But they don't quite stop. Music:*)
What do you think of the USA—NRA—TVA,
What do you think of our Mother's Day,
What do you think of the—

ADMIRALS

Conga!
(*They dance. She attempts to get her interview, but each time the* ADMIRALS *cut in with shrieks of "Conga!" As the number becomes more violent and* RUTH *is hurled about from one* CADET *to the other, she remains grimly resolved to disregard them and get her story.*)

RUTH

What do you think of our native squaws,

WONDERFUL TOWN

Charles G. Dawes,
Warden Lawes—
What's your opinion of Santa Claus,
What do you think of the—

ADMIRALS

Conga!
   (*They dance.*)

RUTH

Good neighbors— Good neighbors,
Remember our policy—
Good neighbors—I'll help you
If you'll just help me—

ADMIRALS

Conga!
   (*They dance.* RUTH *gets more and more involved.*)

RUTH

What's your opinion of Harold Teen,
Mitzi Green,
Dizzy Dean.
Who do you love on the silver screen—
What do you think of the—

ADMIRALS

Conga!
   (*More dancing, with* RUTH *struggling to get out of it.*)

RUTH

What do you think of our rhythm bands,

Monkey glands,
Hot-dog stands.
What do you think of Stokowski's hands—
What do you think of the—

ADMIRALS

Conga!
(*Dance*)

RUTH

Good neighbors— Good neighbors,
Remember our policy—
Good neighbors—I'll help you
If you'll just help me—

ADMIRALS

Conga!
(*By now the dancing is abandoned and wild.*)

RUTH

What's your opinion of women's clothes,
Major Bowes,
Steinbeck's prose.
How do you feel about Broadway Rose—
What do you think of the—

ADMIRALS

Conga!

RUTH

What do you think of our rocks and rills,
Mother Sills sea-sick pills.
How do you feel about Helen Wills—
What do you think of the—

ADMIRALS

Conga!

RUTH

Good neighbors— Good neighbors,
Remember our policy—
Good neighbors—I'll help you
If you'll just help me!!

> (ADMIRALS *sing serenade, strumming on imaginary gui-*
> *tars while* RUTH *stands totally exhausted. They yell*
> *"Conga!" again, and lift her on their backs. Careening*
> *about,* RUTH *still tries to get her interview.*)

Stop!
What do you think of our double malts,
Family vaults,
Epsom Salts,
Wouldn't you guys like to learn to waltz?
I know—You just want to——Conga!

> (*She is whirled about piggy-back in Conga rhythm, her*
> *hat over her eyes—and finally lifted aloft and carried off*
> *stage—as the music builds to a frenetic finish.*)

ACT ONE

Scene VIII

THE BACK YARD. RUTH *enters, immediately after rise, on street, followed by* ADMIRALS.

RUTH

Good night! Au revoir! Auf wiedersehn! Good-bye! (*To* EILEEN, *who enters from studio*) Eileen. Eileen!

EILEEN

What's going on?

RUTH

The Fleet's in!

EILEEN

(*To* ADMIRALS)

How do you do?

RUTH

Listen, Emily Post— How do you say, "Get the hell out of here" in Portuguese?

EILEEN

Why? What's the matter?

RUTH

Suppose *you* take 'em outside and walk 'em around! I'm sick of having kids whistle at me.

EILEEN

You mean they don't understand any English at all?

110

RUTH

Yes—three words—American dance—conga!

A CADET

Conga! Da-da-da-da-da-da!
(*He starts to dance. The others restrain him hastily.*)

RUTH

Listen boys—Go! Leave! Good-bye!
(*She waves.* ADMIRALS *return wave, mutter happily "Goo-bye."* RUTH *turns back to* EILEEN, *shrugs and steps back to her.*)

EILEEN

What did you bring them here for?

RUTH

Bring them! They've been on my tail ever since I left the Brooklyn Navy Yard.

EILEEN

What do they want anyway?

RUTH

What do you *think* they want?

EILEEN

Oh, my God! We've got to get them out of here! Make them go, Ruth!

RUTH

Suppose you take a crack at it.

III

EILEEN
(*Sweetly*)
Look, boys. Go back to your boat. Boat!
(*She salutes.* ADMIRALS *snap to attention, salute in return.*)

RUTH
Admiral Sherwood, I presume.
(*They drop salute.*)

EILEEN
Boys—go way—please!
(*Supplicating—her arms extended—they take it wrongly
—howl and step forward after her.* EILEEN *shrieks, runs
back to* RUTH.)

RUTH
That's fine.

EILEEN
Gee, they can't be *that* dumb.

RUTH
They're *not* that dumb.

EILEEN
What are we going to do?

RUTH
I've tried everything. I guess, Eileen, we'll just have to stand
here grinning at each other.
(*She turns to* ADMIRALS *and grins broadly.* ADMIRALS *all
grin back. She motions helplessly, steps back in to*
EILEEN.)

112

EILEEN

Look—boys—sick! Very sick! (*Sits on bench—leans all the way back—on "bed"*) Bed! Bed!
> (*The* ADMIRALS *rush in at her.* EILEEN *jumps up, shrieks, makes a dash for* RUTH, *swings behind her for protection.*)

RUTH

For God's sake, don't let 'em get any wrong ideas!

EILEEN

You brought them here! The least you can do is help me get rid of them! (*The* ADMIRALS *start to toss coins*) What are they tossing for?

RUTH

I don't know, but I've got a hunch it's not me!
> (*An* ADMIRAL *goes to them gravely.*)

FIRST ADMIRAL
(*Bowing*)

Senorita, eu tive e grande prazer de a ganhar esta noite.

RUTH

Isn't it a romantic language?

EILEEN

No understando—no spikee Portuguese—

FIRST CADET

American dance—Conga!
> (*He turns* EILEEN, *takes her by the wrist and other*

ADMIRALS *join in.* RUTH *dances backwards, in front of*
EILEEN.)

RUTH

Eileen, we've got to get them out of here.
(*There is a blast from below. The* ADMIRALS *stop and
cross themselves in fear.*)

EILEEN

Run—Earthquake!
(EILEEN *runs to doorway, hides against it, to see if* AD-
MIRALS *disperse.* ADMIRALS *make for the stairway.* WAIT-
ERS *and* CHEF *enter from* NINO'S. *Passers-by stop on the
street to stare down. The* ADMIRALS *stop on steps, look
at one another and laugh.*)

RUTH

What a performance! Helen Hayes couldn't have done better. Listen, I've got an idea. Lead 'em out through the alley
and lose them on the street!

EILEEN

Okay, but tell Bob I'll be right back.

RUTH

Bob?

EILEEN

Yes, I'm having dinner with him. (*To* ADMIRALS) Come on,
boys—Conga!
(*Boys make line.* EILEEN *exits into alley,* ADMIRALS *Con-
gaing after her.* RUTH *stares off unhappily. The* WAITERS
from NINO'S *start to Conga gaily.* BAKER *enters from street*

and looks strangely at CHEF *and two* WAITERS *in Conga
line. He goes to* RUTH.)

Ruth, what's going on?

RUTH
(*Looks at him and starts to Conga by herself*)
Oh, a few friends dropped in. We're losing our inhibitions!
(*She grabs piece of celery from* WAITER, *puts it between
her teeth, starts to Conga wildly. She starts her own
line, with* CHEF, *and* WAITERS *following. As they go off
they are met by* EILEEN *coming back, still followed by
the* ADMIRALS *and a huge snake line of mixed* VILLAGERS.
RUTH *backs away, in dismay.*)

EILEEN
I couldn't lose them!
(MRS. WADE *comes on with* LONIGAN *and another cop.
Whistles are blown by* LONIGAN. *Meanwhile* RUTH *has
been hoisted up in the air by* ADMIRALS. COP *makes a grab
for* EILEEN, *picks her up. She turns in the air, kicks*
LONIGAN *in the stomach. He drags her off.* MRS. WADE
*has made for the stairs and stands on the first landing,
motioning wildly.* RUTH *gets down from her perch and
desperately starts to run across after* EILEEN. *She is grabbed
by one of the* ADMIRALS, *carried, slid back and overhead
by the* ADMIRALS. BAKER *runs after* EILEEN *as* RUTH *is conga-
ed aloft amidst a swirl of village figures, all caught up in
the frenzy of the Conga rhythm.*)

(*Curtain*)

ACT TWO

ACT TWO

SCENE I

THE CHRISTOPHER STREET STATION HOUSE. *A couple of* COPS *are talking as* WRECK *and* HELEN *enter.* WRECK *is carrying a dress of* EILEEN'S.

COP

Hey, what are you doing in here?

HELEN

Good morning.

WRECK

Can we see Miss Sherwood, please?

COP

What do you think this is, the Barbizon Plaza? Miss Who?

HELEN

Eileen Sherwood.

COP

Eileen? Why didn't you say so? (*Calls off stage*) Oh, Eileen!

EILEEN

(*Off stage*)

Yes? What is it, Dennis? (*Enters. Sees* WRECK *and* HELEN. *She is carrying a malted milk*) Oh, hello, Wreck—Helen—

WRECK

Hi, Eileen!

HELEN

The Wreck ironed this dress especially. He thought you'd want to look fresh in court.

EILEEN
(*Taking dress*)
Oh, thanks, Wreck. That's awfully sweet of you. (*To* COP) Dennis—

COP

Yeah, Eileen.

EILEEN
(*Hands dress to him*)
Dennis, would you mind hanging this up in my cell?

COP

Sure, Eileen.
(*He goes off, holding dress carefully over arm.* SECOND COP *enters.*)

SECOND COP

Oh, Eileen.

EILEEN

Yes, Dan—

SECOND COP

There's a man on the phone—wants to talk to you—says it's important.

EILEEN

Who is it, Dan?

SECOND COP

Chick Clark. Says he knows you.

120

EILEEN
(*Angrily*)
You tell Mr. Clark I'm not in to him and hang up on him
if he ever calls again!

SECOND COP
Leave it to me, Eileen.
(*He pats her shoulder and goes.*)

HELEN
(*To* WRECK)
And we were worried about her!

EILEEN
Oh, I'm fine. How are you two getting along?

WRECK
Pretty good. If everything works out all right we'll be leavin'
on our honeymoon next week.

EILEEN
Congratulations! Are you getting married?

HELEN
We decided not to wait for the football season.

WRECK
Yeah. Ya see, Helen went to the doctor—

HELEN
(*Turns to him*)
Wreck!

WRECK

Anyway, the decision was taken out of our hands.

HELEN

Yes, we've got a plan and Appopolous is puttin' up all the dough.

EILEEN

Appopolous!

HELEN

Yes, as soon as I collect my dowry, he'll get his back rent.

EILEEN

Good luck. I hope you'll be very happy.

WRECK

Well, we've been happy so far—I don't see why marriage should change it.
(*They go off.*)

EILEEN
(*To* COP)

And to think I was always afraid of being arrested!

THIRD COP

Ah, that Lonigan's a bum sport— Just because you kicked him!

FOURTH COP
(*Enters*)

Eileen, there's a girl outside—claims she's your sister—

EILEEN

Ruth? Send her in please!
(COP *waves* RUTH *on.*)

122

RUTH

(*Embracing* EILEEN *tearfully*)

Eileen! Oh, you poor kid!

EILEEN

(*Startled*)

What happened?

RUTH

What do you mean, what happened? This!

EILEEN

Oh— Oh, yes—this!

RUTH

I've been all over New York, trying to raise your bail—
Maybe I'd better send a wire to Dad.

EILEEN

Gee, don't do that! He'll ask a lot of foolish questions—

RUTH

Well, we've got to do something.

EILEEN

I'm all right! Everybody's very sweet to me here!

FIRST COP

(*Enters*)

Phone, Eileen.

EILEEN

Who is it, Dennis?

FIRST COP

A Mr. Lippencott. He'd like to know when he can call on you.

EILEEN
(*Thoughtfully*)
Tell him—any time before five.

RUTH
(*Stares*)
Tell me, Eileen, how many do you keep in help here?

EILEEN

Huh?

RUTH

I just love the way you've done this place. Well, I've got to get to work!

EILEEN

Where?

RUTH

The Village Vortex. Your old pal Speedy Valenti gave me a job.

EILEEN

Doing what?

RUTH
(*Hesitates*)
Well, it pays—

FOURTH COP
(*Enters*)
Eileen, there's a gentleman to see you.
(*Hands* EILEEN *a business card.*)

EILEEN
(*Reading*)
Robert Baker! Why, it's *Bob*! Send him in, please.

RUTH
(*Turning unhappily*)
I'd better go.

BAKER
(*Enters*)
How are you, Eileen? (*Turns to* RUTH) Oh, hello, Ruth—

RUTH
(*Flatly*)
Hello.

BAKER
What happened to you, Ruth?,I looked for you after the patrol wagon left.

RUTH
I went for a walk—had a lot of things to think over—

BAKER
You do look a little tired.

RUTH
I am. I didn't sleep all night—(*To* EILEEN)—worrying about *you*— So I sat at that typewriter and wrote the story about the Brazilian Admirals. It's a darn good story—I know it is! I took your advice—a slice of my own life—and I sent it to Chick's city editor—Mr. Bains. (*Sadly*) But they didn't print it, so I guess it wasn't so good after all—

125

BAKER

Want *me* to read it?

RUTH

If you feel up to it—(*To* EILEEN) Sorry to eat and run, darling—but I've got to get to work!
(*Kisses her.*)

BAKER

(*To* RUTH)
Did you get a job? What are you doing?

RUTH

Oh, it's in the advertising game. (*Looks at wrist watch*) Cocktail time, already? Well, I've got to fly! 'Bye, dear—lovely party—such fun! *Do* ask me again!
(*She hurries off.*)

EILEEN

Poor Ruth! I didn't have the heart to tell her. There isn't any Mr. Bains—

BAKER

What?

EILEEN

It was all a big lie! That Chick Clark's an utter snake! Oh, if I could only get out of here, I'd—

BAKER

Look, I'm working on this. I'm going to get you out. I just tried to pay your fine, but they haven't set it yet.

EILEEN

Why not?
126

BAKER

I don't know. Washington wants them to hold you here.

EILEEN
(*Gasps*)

Washington—D.C.?

BAKER

Something about Pan-American relations.

EILEEN

Oh, my God!

BAKER

But don't worry—I'm working on this.

FOURTH COP
(*Entering, making a butler's announcement*)

Frank Lippencott.

EILEEN

Send him in, Pat.

BAKER

I'm going over to see the Brazilian Consul right now.
(*He starts out.* FRANK *enters. They collide.* FRANK *carries small box.*)

FRANK

Oops! Sorry—(BAKER *exits irritatedly.* FRANK *combs his hair quickly*) Gee, this is the first time I was ever in a police station.

EILEEN

It's *my* first time, too.

LIPPENCOTT

I brought you an electric fan we're running. I thought it
would cool off your cell.
(*Holds box out to her.*)

EILEEN

Isn't that thoughtful!

LIPPENCOTT

It's given away free with every purchase over five dollars.

EILEEN

Thanks.

FRANK
(*Opening box*)

Somebody forgot it.

EILEEN

You're sweet.

FRANK
(*Removing small rubber fan from box*)

You'd be surprised at the breeze that little thing gives off—
(*He spins blade, holds it up to* EILEEN's *face*) Everybody in the
store's got a cold.
(*He hands her fan.* FOURTH COP *enters.*)

EILEEN
(*To* COP)

Pat, would you mind putting these things in my cell?
(*She gets suitcase, hands it to* ANDERSON.)

128

FOURTH COP

Yes, sure.

EILEEN

Thank you.

(FOURTH COP *exits.*)

FRANK

Eileen, I want to ask you something—it's the most important decision I ever made in my life—

EILEEN

Frank, you're a very sweet boy, and I'm fond of you, but I'm really not thinking of getting married.

FRANK

No, neither am I.

EILEEN

You're not?

FRANK

No.

EILEEN

Then what are you thinking of?

FRANK

Listen, Eileen—I suddenly realize I've been wasting my life—

EILEEN

What are you talking about?

FRANK

You know—*Life*—the way you girls live it—free to follow your natural bent whatever it is—

129

EILEEN

What's all that got to do with me?

FRANK

Don't you see? We'd have our freedom and we'd have each other. I thought we could have a sort of ideal relationship, like · Helen and The Wreck—

EILEEN
(*Aghast*)

Timothy!

FRANK

Gee, Eileen, it was only an idea!

EILEEN

Show this gentleman out—and don't ever let him in here again!
(*He goes quickly. As he passes* COP, COP *stamps his foot menacingly.* FRANK *quickens speed, exits.*)

FIFTH COP
(*Enters excitedly*)

Eileen! Did you see the paper?

EILEEN

No.

FIFTH COP

Look! You're in it!

FIRST COP
(*Enters*)

Eileen's in the papers.

130

FIFTH COP

A big story! Your picture and everything!

EILEEN

Oh, for goodness sakes!

FOURTH COP
(*Comes in with others*)
Hey! That's me! Not bad, huh?

FIRST COP

That jerk Lonigan has his back to the camera! He'll fry!

SECOND COP

Look, Lonigan!
(LONIGAN *enters*.)

FOURTH COP

You're famous, Eileen!

EILEEN

Do you think so? I wonder if Mr. Valenti saw it? (*To* LON-IGAN) Oh, John, it's on your beat. Would you do me a great favor? Would you take this over to the Village Vortex and show it to Speedy Valenti personally?

THIRD COP

He'd better!

LONIGAN

Sure, Eileen. I'll serve it on him!

131

THIRD COP

Atta boy, John! (*To* EILEEN *as music begins*) Oh, Eileen, you brought a breath of the old country into the station house.

FOURTH COP

(*In greatly exaggerated Irish brogue*)
Sure and I been feelin' twice as Irish since you came into our lives.
(*Singing à la John McCormack*)

Take it from me,
In Dublin's fair city
There's none half so pretty
As pretty Eileen.

Take it from me,
The Mayor of Shannon
Would shoot off a cannon
And crown ye the queen.

ALL

Darlin' Eileen,
Darlin' Eileen,
Fairest colleen that iver I've seen.
And it's oh I wish I were back in the land of the green
With my darlin' Eileen.

FIRST COP

I've seen them all—
There's Bridget and Sheila

132

SECOND COP

There's Kate and Deli—lah
And Moll and Maureen.

THIRD COP

I've seen them all—
Not one can compete with—

FIRST COP

Or share the same street with
My darlin' Eileen.

ALL

Darlin' Eileen— Darlin' Eileen,
Fairest colleen
That iver I've seen—
And it's oh I wish I were back
In the land of the green
With my darlin' Eileen.
   (*They dance a lusty jig of the Old Country, lumbering
   but full of life, all vying for her attention.*)

EILEEN

   (*Somewhat apprehensive, cutting them off*)
Listen, my lads,
I've something to tell you
I hope won't impel you to cry and to keen.
Mother's a Swede and Father's a Scot—
And so Irish I'm not— And I never have been—

ALL

   (*They will not hear of this*)
Hush you, Eileen! Hush you, Eileen!

133

Fairest colleen that iver I've seen.
Don't you hand us none of that blarney—
You come from Killarney,
You're Irish, Eileen!
(*The dance resumes and ends in a "hats-off" salute to the girl of their dreams,* EILEEN.)

(*Blackout*)

ACT TWO

Scene II

THE STREET. AT RISE: MRS. WADE *sitting on a camp stool, posing;* APPOPOLOUS *painting her picture.*

MRS. WADE

May I look?

APPOPOLOUS

No, it's still an embryo. Let it kick and breathe first. As a model you will be immortalized like Van Gogh's herring!

(*The* WRECK *and* HELEN *enter.* HELEN *pushes him in. He wears navy-blue suit, carries hat. She motions to his head. He puts hat on, starts to step in.* HELEN *grabs him, motions to glasses. He puts bone glasses on.* HELEN *goes off as* WRECK *crosses to* APPOPOLOUS *and looks over his shoulder at canvas.*)

WRECK

Bravo! Magnificent! You've captured the inner soul of this lovely lady!

APPOPOLOUS

Thank you, Mr. Loomis. (MRS. WADE *looks at* WRECK) That's indeed a compliment coming from a great collector like you!

WRECK

Not at all!

APPOPOLOUS

May I present you? Mr. Loomis—Mrs. Wade—

MRS. WADE

Pleased to meet you.

WRECK

(*Removing his hat*)

I'm delighted. Maestro, I'd like to add this to my collection. Is it for sale?

APPOPOLOUS

Sorry! I'm presenting this to Mrs. Wade!

(HELEN *enters.*)

HELEN

Hello, Mother.

MRS. WADE

Oh, Helen. Come here a moment! I want you to meet someone! This is my daughter, Helen—Mr. Loomis.

WRECK

Daughter? You're spoofing! You look more like sisters!

HELEN

I'm very pleased to meet you, Mr. Loomis.

WRECK

Likewise, I'm sure! Well, this is delightful! May I invite you all to tea at the Purple Cow?

MRS. WADE

Oh.

136

APPOPOLOUS

Fine! You young people go along, and we'll join you in a minute.

(WRECK *smiles, offers his arm to* HELEN. *She takes it.*)

HELEN

Do you get down to the Village very often, Mr. Loomis?

(*They go off.*)

MRS. WADE

Who *is* he?

APPOPOLOUS

He comes from a very aristocratic family from Trenton Tech.

(APPOPOLOUS *and* MRS. WADE *go off.* RUTH *enters with* MAN *with sign. As passers-by come on, they turn on electric signs reading* "VORTEX" *across their chests.*)

RUTH

(*To* MAN)

I feel like a damn fool!

MAN

(*Shrugs*)

It's a living.

(*Another couple passes by.* RUTH *and* MAN *turn on signs.*)

VILLAGER

You ever been there?

SECOND VILLAGER

Yeah, last night.

(*They go off.*)

137

RUTH

I'm really a writer, you know.

MAN

I'm really an architect, but they haven't built anything since
the Empire State Building.

RUTH
(*Spotting someone off stage*)
Oh, this is awful!

MAN

What's the matter?

RUTH

Here comes someone I know! Please, don't light up!

MAN

Sure! Don't worry about it.
(RUTH *turns, faces* MAN, *simulates fixing his tie.* BAKER
enters. After he has passed RUTH, *she and* MAN *turn and
stroll off.* BAKER *recognizes* RUTH, *turns.*)

BAKER

Ruth!

RUTH
(*Turns, brightly*)
Oh, hello there!
(*Hastily she folds her arms across the electric sign.*)

BAKER

Well, this is a surprise! Going out?

138

RUTH

Yes, we are—to the opera. Mr. Stevens, I'd like you to meet Mr. Baker. Mr. Stevens is in Washington with the Reconstruction Finance Corporation.

(*They shake.*)

BAKER

(*To* RUTH)

I read your piece about the Brazilian Navy. Now that's the idea! It's fine!

RUTH

Really? No repressions? No inhibitions?

BAKER

No, just good clean fun. I gave it to the boss to read. I'm sure he'll go for it.

RUTH

Oh, thank you, Bob. That's wonderful of you!

(VALENTI *enters.*)

MAN

(*To* RUTH)

Hey, Ruth, we're going to be late for the opera!

RUTH

Just a minute, please. This is important!

MAN

So is this! More important!

(*Points to* VALENTI.)

VALENTI

What's going on here? Get on the ball! (MAN *snaps light on,*

BAKER *stares in wonder.* RUTH *looks at him unhappily.*) Well?
What's with you, sister—run out of juice?

RUTH
(Lights up and smiles feebly at BAKER)
Well, it's a healthy job. Keeps me out in the air!

BAKER
(Pats her arm reassuringly)
Good girl.
(He smiles at her and goes off.)

VALENTI
No socializing on my time. *(Goes to* MAN) Here's a pitch.
You take Sheridan Square. *(Hands flyer to* MAN *who exits and
then hands her flyer)* Here's your spiel—come on, get a mob
around you. Make with the pitch. Get hep.
*(*VALENTI *exits.)*

RUTH
(Tentatively)
Yes, sir—hep. *(Reading from flyer—very tentatively to pass-
ers-by)* Step up—step up—*(Embarrassed)* Get hep—get hep—
(Suddenly, loudly)
Step up!
(Rhythm starts in orchestra. RUTH *still reading from flyer,
giving a very "square" rendition.)*
Step up! Step up!
Get hep! Get hep!
*(While she reads a crowd of '30's hepcats gathers around
her.)*
Come on down to the Village Vortex

WONDERFUL TOWN

Home of the new jazz rage—Swing!
Rock and roll to the beat beat beat
Of Speedy Valenti and his krazy kats!
(Sings falteringly)
Swing! Dig the rhythm!
Swing! Dig the message!
The jive is jumpin' and the music goes around and around—
Whoa-ho—!
Goes around and around—
Cat, make it solid!
Cat, make it groovy!
You gotta get your seafood, Mama, your favorite dish is fish,
It's your favorite dish.
Don't be square,
Rock right out of that rockin' chair;
Truck on down and let down your hair;
Breathe that barrel-house air!
The Village Vortex!
Swing! Dig the rhythm!
Swing! Dig the message!
The jive is jumpin' and the music goes around and around—
Get full of foory-a-ka-sa-ke,
Get full of the sound of swing,
The solid, jivy, groovy sound of swing!

HEPCATS
(Singing and showing RUTH how to get hep)
Swing! Dig the rhythm!
Swing! Dig the message!
The jive is jumpin' and the music goes around and around—
Whoa-ho—!

RUTH

(*Getting the idea*)

Oh!

VILLAGERS

Cat, make it solid!
Cat, make it groovy!
You gotta get your seafood, Mama;
Your favorite dish is fish—

RUTH

(*Catching on still more and beginning to enjoy it*)
Oh!

VILLAGERS

Don't be square,
Rock right out of that rockin' chair;
Truck on down and let down your hair;
Breathe that barrel-house air—
You gotta get with the whoa-ho-de-ho!

RUTH

(*Answering Cab Calloway fashion*)
Whoa-ho-de-ho.

VILLAGERS

The gut-gut-bucket.

RUTH

The gut-gut-bucket.

VILLAGERS

Skid-dle-ee-oh-day!

RUTH

Skid-dle-ee-oh-day!

142

WONDERFUL TOWN

Heedle heedle heedle.

RUTH

Heedle heedle heedle.

VILLAGERS

Well, all right then, cats!

RUTH

Well, all right then, cats!

VILLAGERS

Yes, yes, baby I know!

RUTH

(By this time RUTH *is in a glaze-eyed hypnotic trance, having got the message and as the hepcats gather around her she delivers patter in a husky dreamlike monotone)*

Well, yes yes, baby, I know!
That old man Mose
Kicked the bucket,
The old oaken bucket that hung in the well—
Well, well, well, baby, I know—
No no; was it red?
No no no! Was it green green—
Green is the color of my true love's hair—
Hair-breadth Harry with the floy floy doy
Floy doy, floy doy, floy doy, hoy!
Hoy dre(h)eamt hoy dwe(h)elt in ma(h)arble halls—
Well that ends well, well, well—
Baby I know—No, no,
Was it green?
No no no
Was it red sails in the sunset callin'-me me me
You good for nothin'

143

Mi-mi mi-mi
Me Tarzan, you Jane,
Swingin' in the trees,
Swingin' in the trees,
Swingin' in the trees—
(*This develops into an abandoned dance in which* RUTH *not only joins but finally leads the hepcats to a "sent" finish.*)

VILLAGERS

Swing—swing—swing—swing—swing—swing
Swing—Chu-chu-chu chu-chu-chu chu-chu-chu-chu
Swing—Chu-chu-chu chu-chu-chu chu-chu-chu-chu
Swing—Chu-chu-chu chu-chu-chu chu-chu-chu-chu

RUTH

Floy-doy floy-doy floy-doy hoy!

VILLAGERS

Sh-sh-sh.

RUTH

Gesundheit.

VILLAGERS

Thanks.

RUTH

You're welcome.

VILLAGERS

Whoa!
(*Motioning to* RUTH)
Come on, Jackson, you're getting hep.

Come on, Jackson, you're getting hep.
Come on, Jackson, you're getting hep.

RUTH

I want my favorite dish.

VILLAGERS

Fish.

RUTH

Gesundheit.

VILLAGERS

Thanks.

RUTH

It's nothing!

VILLAGERS

Solid, groovy, jivy sound of swing—

FIRST MAN

Ah—do it.

SECOND MAN

Solid, Jackson.

FIRST GIRL

Seafood, Mama.

SECOND GIRL

(*A long banshee wail*)

VILLAGERS

Go go go—yah—
Swing—oh swing it,
Swing—oh swing it.

WONDERFUL TOWN

(*The dance continues, as the* VILLAGERS *back out, followed by* RUTH *in a trance.*)

RUTH

(*In a hoarse, hypnotic whisper*)
Swing— Swing
Green, no—red, no
Me Tarzan— No, no, no
That old man Mose
He kicked that bucket
Down in the well—well, well, well
My favorite dish
Ahhh—fish!

VILLAGERS

Gesundheit.

RUTH

Thank you.

VILLAGERS

You're welcome.

RUTII

(*Her hands before her, mesmerized. Walks off in a trance*)
Swing—swing—swing—swing—swing—
(*She disappears.*)

(*Blackout*)

ACT TWO

Scene III

THE STUDIO. AT RISE: *Stage empty. Through window, VIO-LET's legs pass by, then man's legs. VIOLET stops, half turns. Man comes back and joins her. They stand, then go off together.*

(During this scene, APPOPOLOUS enters carrying blue-green painting. He steps on bed, looks about for something to stand on, picks up manuscripts off typewriter next to bed, and slips one under each foot. He hangs painting, jumps down, takes valise from under RUTH's bed, puts it on top of bed, takes type-writer from chair next to bed, puts it on bed, gets books and candlesticks off and puts them on bed. RUTH enters from bath-room in her slip. She screams.)

RUTH

Ah! What are you doing with my things?
(She takes robe from bathroom and slips it on.)

APPOPOLOUS

You're being dispossessed! I only hope your sister has sense enough to give the wrong address!

RUTH

Yes, imagine what bad publicity could do to this dump!

APPOPOLOUS

(Pointing to painting)
I found my masterpiece in Benny's. For the frame, two dol-

lars—for my painting, nothing! At six o'clock your current occupancy terminates! (*Knock on door*) Remember! If you're not out by the stroke of six, you'll find your belongings in the street!

(*He goes out through kitchen. There is another knock on the door.*)

RUTH

Come in. (BAKER *enters*) Oh, Bob—

BAKER

(*Sadly*)

Oh, hello, Ruth.

RUTH

What's the matter?

BAKER

(*Angrily*)

All I can say is, he wouldn't know a good story if he read one!

RUTH

Who?

BAKER

His Highness—king of the editors—pompous ass.

(APPOPOLOUS *sticks head in from kitchen door.*)

APPOPOLOUS

Fifteen minutes!

(*Disappears again.*)

BAKER

What was *that*?

148

RUTH

Bulova Watch Time.

BAKER

I'm sorry, Ruth. He just didn't like it.

RUTH
(Shrugs)
Well, maybe it wasn't any good.

BAKER

It's just one man's opinion.

RUTH

That's enough.

BAKER

I still think it's a hell of a good story and I'm going to tell
him so!

RUTH

Please, Bob, don't get into any trouble on my account.

BAKER

This has nothing to do with you. It's a matter of principle.
Either I know my business or I don't!

RUTH
(Nods slowly)
I see.
(EILEEN *enters from street with* LONIGAN, *who is carrying
her suitcase.*)
EILEEN

Ruth!

RUTH
(*Embracing her*)
Eileen! Darling, you're out! How did it happen?

EILEEN
Bob fixed everything. Thanks, Bob.
(CHICK CLARK *appears at window*.)

CHICK
Hello, kids.

EILEEN
Chick Clark! You get away from there, you big snake!

CHICK
Now wait a minute, Eileen! Gimme a chance.

EILEEN
You had enough chances!

RUTH
What are you talking about?

EILEEN
Ruth, when I tell you what he did—

CHICK
Wait! The city editor's read your Brazilian story and he
thinks it's the absolute nuts!

RUTH
(*Going to window. Hopefully*)
He does?

150

EILEEN

Don't believe him, Ruth! He's the biggest liar!

CHICK

Go ahead—call him up! Mr. Wilson! You know the number!

RUTH

Wilson? I thought his name was Bains?

EILEEN

You see, Ruth, he's lying again! (*To* LONIGAN) John, will you do me a great favor and chase him away from there?

LONIGAN

Glad to!
(*He runs out.*)

CHICK

Now wait a minute, Eileen. You're gonna louse it up! Tell her to call Mr. Wilson—the city editor—I keep tellin' her all the time!
(CHICK *runs off as* LONIGAN *stops at window.*)

LONIGAN

(*Kneels down, offering her whistle*)
Oh, Eileen, if anything else happens, here's a police whistle.

EILEEN

(*Taking whistle*)
Thanks, John.
(LONIGAN *goes.*)

151

RUTH

Next week you'll have your own hook and ladder.

APPOPOLOUS

(*Sticking head through kitchen*)

Five minutes!

EILEEN

What's that about?

RUTH

We're being dispossessed.

BAKER

Where are you going?

RUTH

(*Hands* EILEEN *suitcase*)

I don't know—home, I guess.

EILEEN

We can't. What would people say?

RUTH

"Did you hear the dirt about those Sherwood girls? On account of them, we almost lost the Naval Base in Brazil."

BAKER

It's ridiculous. You can't go home now.

RUTH

But, Bob—

BAKER

I haven't time to argue about it. (*Looks at his watch*) I've got to get up to the office before His Highness leaves. He wants to see me—and I want to see him a damn sight more! (*Goes to door*) Now I want you to promise me you'll wait right here till I get back.

RUTH

You'd better hurry, or you may find us out in the street.

BAKER

Half an hour. Top.
  (*He's off.*)

EILEEN

Isn't he nice?

RUTH

(*Sits on bed wearily*)
Um—You like him a lot, don't you, Eileen?

EILEEN

You know, Ruth, he's the first boy I've ever met who really seemed to care what happened to me—how I got along and everything.

RUTH

Yes, I know. (*Shrugs*) I guess it doesn't make any difference now anyway—

EILEEN

What?

RUTH

(*Close to tears*)
I said we're going home—so it doesn't matter about Bob.

153

EILEEN

(*Goes slowly to* RUTH, *putting an arm around her*)
Gee, Ruth, I never dreamed. You mean you like him too?

RUTH

Strange as it may seem—

EILEEN

Well, why didn't you say anything?

RUTH

What was there to say?

EILEEN

After all—you're my sister.

RUTH

(*Smiles at her through her tears*)
That's the side of you that makes everything else seem worth-while.

EILEEN

Gee, Ruth—I'm sorry we ever came here.
(*Puts her head on* RUTH's *shoulder.*)

BOTH

Why, oh why, oh why—oh
Why did we ever leave Ohio?
Why did we wander to find what lies yonder
When life was so cozy at home?

Wond'ring while we wander,
Why did we fly,

154

Why did we roam—
Oh, why oh why oh
Did we leave Ohio?
Maybe we'd better go home.
(APPOPOLOUS *enters.*)

APPOPOLOUS

Time's up! Your occupancy is officially terminated.

RUTH

We're not ready yet.
(VALENTI *enters.*)

VALENTI

Skeet—skat—skattle-ee-o-do! (*He carries newspaper*) Where is she? I know it! I said it! I meant it! You hit me in my weak spot—(*Slaps newspaper*) Right on the front page!

EILEEN

Oh, Mr. Valenti! How did you like it?

RUTH

(*Takes newspaper, reading headline*)
Like what? "Beautiful Blonde Bombshell Sinks Brazilian Navy." Oh, my—now we *can't* go home!

VALENTI

(*To* EILEEN)
You're in the groove, babe! I'm gonna put you in my saloon for an audition tonight. If you make good, I'll sign you!

155

EILEEN

Oh, Mr. Valenti! Speedy! That's wonderful! (*To* RUTH)
Ruth, it's a job! My first break in the theatre.
(*They embrace.*)

APPOPOLOUS

Girls, I'm gonna extend your time until six o'clock tomorrow
morning. Make good and you can be with me for life!
(*He goes.*)

VALENTI

(*To* EILEEN)

Get over there right away!

EILEEN

Yes, yes. (*To* RUTH) Only what about Bob?

RUTH

We'll leave a note on the door.

EILEEN

What'll I wear, Mr. Valenti?

VALENTI

I'll lend you a dress. I'll lend your sister one too—(RUTH *looks
up*)—and without the lights. Now get over there. (*Goes to
door*) What are you gonna sing, Babe?

EILEEN

Ruth, remember the song we always used to do at the Kiwanis Club? The Wrong Note Rag?

156

RUTH

Oh, yes—do that one.

VALENTI

It's an oldie, but you'll never know it when I back you up with the licorice stick.

RUTH

The what?

VALENTI

My clarinet. Then for an encore— Tell me, kid—did you ever take 'em off?

EILEEN

What?

VALENTI

You know, *strip?*

RUTH

My sister doesn't strip.

VALENTI

Too bad. We're always looking for new faces!

(*Blackout*)

ACT TWO

Scene IV

THE STREET *in front of the* VORTEX. AT RISE: HELEN *and*
WRECK *enter, followed by* MRS. WADE *and* APPOPOLOUS.

HELEN

That was a lovely dinner, Mr. Loomis!

APPOPOLOUS
(Grimly)

Yes, he's certainly a fine host—everything out of season!

WRECK

Why not? You only live once!

APPOPOLOUS

Only the champagne I didn't expect!

MRS. WADE

It's good, though! Hit the spot!

WRECK

There! You see, Maestro?

HELEN

Come on! Let's get a good table!

158

WRECK

Yeah.

(*They go off.* APPOPOLOUS *takes* MRS. WADE's *arm.*)

APPOPOLOUS

One moment, Ella. They make a lovely couple, don't they?

MRS. WADE

Yes! Do you think his intentions are serious?

APPOPOLOUS

I'll vouch for it.

MRS. WADE

Did you notice he was holding Helen's hand under the table? My, I'd love to see my Helen settled down!

APPOPOLOUS

(*Offers his arm*)

Don't worry, Ella, she'll be settled down and you'll be a grandmother before you expect it!

(*They go off.* RUTH *and* EILEEN *hurry on.*)

EILEEN

Oh, dear, I'm so frightened!

RUTH

Now look, Eileen, you're not afraid of anything. I know you better than that!

EILEEN

You do?

(CHICK CLARK *runs on.*)

159

CHICK

Hey, kids! I gotta talk to you!

EILEEN

Chick Clark, for the last time, stop annoying us!

CHICK

I tell ya! I got it all fixed!

EILEEN

All right! You asked for it—now you're going to get it!
(*She puts whistle, attached to her wrist, to her lips and
blows several times.*)

CHICK

What are you doin'? Ya crazy!
(LONIGAN *dashes on,* CHICK *runs off.* EILEEN *points in*
CHICK's *direction.* LONIGAN *follows him off.*)

RUTH

Eileen, are you sure you're doing the right thing?

EILEEN

Some day I'll tell you the truth about Mr. Chick Clark!
(*Clutches her stomach*) Oh, gee—I'm all upset again! I feel
nauseous!

RUTH

You do? Well, look—walk up and down in the air—and
breathe deeply— That's right. I'll take your case and get you
some black coffee.
(*She goes off.*)

EILEEN

Oh, thanks, Ruth.
(BAKER *enters with piece of paper.*)

BAKER

Eileen—I found your note—this is wonderful news!
(*Takes her hands.*)

EILEEN

Thanks, Bob.

BAKER

Now, no more of that nonsense about going home.

EILEEN

Oh, no. No.

BAKER

And I'll get something for Ruth—just as soon as I land a job
myself.

EILEEN

Job! What happened?

BAKER

Well, I left the *Manhatter*—uh—a difference of opinion—

EILEEN

Oh, Bob—I'm awfully sorry— But I think it's wonderful that
you feel that way about Ruth!

BAKER

Well, I'm very fond of her—

EILEEN

Fond? It must be more than that if you got fired on her account.

BAKER

I left on a matter of principle!

EILEEN

Principle! Don't play dumb!

BAKER

Dumb?

EILEEN

Well, you must be if you don't know what's going on in your own mind!

BAKER

Will you please tell me what's going on in my mind?

EILEEN

I suppose you don't know why you fought with your editor about Ruth's story—or why you're picking a fight with me right now! Poor Bob—you're in love with Ruth and you don't even know it!
(*Sings.*)
It's love! It's love!

BAKER

(*Sings*)
Come on now— Let's drop it.

EILEEN

It's love! It's love! ′
And nothing can stop it.

162

BAKER

You're a silly girl— It's a sign of youth.

EILEEN

(*Shakes head*)

You're a silly boy— You're in love with Ruth.
It's love! It's love!
Come on now— Just try it.

BAKER

(*Tentatively*)

It's love! It's love!

EILEEN

Don't try to deny it,
I know the signs,
I know it when I see it—
So just face it,
Just say it.

BAKER

It's love,
It's love,
    (BAKER *sings*—BIG.)
It's love!!
    (EILEEN *watches him a moment—then exits.*)
Maybe— It's love! It's love!
    (*As the realization grows.*)
Well, who would have thought it
If this is love,
Then why have I fought it?
What a way to feel—

163

I could touch the sky.
What a way to feel—
I'm a different guy!

It's love, at last,
I've someone to cheer for—
It's love, at last,
I've learned what we're here for—
I've heard it said,
"You'll know it when you see it."
Well, I see it—I know it—
It's Love!
    (*Exits happily.*)

ACT TWO

SCENE V

THE VILLAGE VORTEX, *a surrealistic night club, hung with paintings from every artist who couldn't pay his tab, and dominated by a huge revolving mobile, hung from the ceiling.* VALENTI *leads the band with his clarinet as the crowd dances a slow, writhing jitterbug, packed tightly together like anchovies.*

VALENTI
(*As dance ends and a bedlam of sound from the crowd bubbles up*)
Settle down! Settle down!
    (WRECK *has opened bottle of champagne. Rises with bottle and glass.*)

WRECK
Folks, here's a toast to my future mother-in-law. Long may she wave!

PATRON
(*From balcony*)
Sit down, you bum!
    (WRECK *starts to remove his coat and glasses, shakes an angry fist at patron.*)

HELEN
(*To* WRECK)
Please, Mr. Loomis—
    (WRECK *subsides.*)

165

VALENTI

Cat and Gates! You've read about her, you've talked about
her! Now here she is in person, fresh from a cellar in Christopher Street—Miss Eileen Sherwood!

(RUTH *and* EILEEN *enter.* RUTH *is pushing* EILEEN, *fixing
her hair at the last minute.*)

Give the little girl a great big hand!

(*He leads applause.* EILEEN *climbs steps*—RUTH *sits on
bottom step.*)

CHICK

(*Enters*)

Hey, Ruth, I gotta square myself with you.

RUTH

Go away—my sister's going to sing!

EILEEN

You get out of here, Chick Clark!

FRANK

(*Stepping in*)

Is he annoying you, Miss Sherwood?

CHICK

(*Pushing* FRANK)

Go on back to your drugstore! No! Look, Ruth! I got your
press card, signed by the city editor! You start Monday!

RUTH

Is it true?

166

CHICK

It's official—I tell ya!

LONIGAN

(*To* CHICK)

All right you—come on!
(*Takes* CHICK's *arm.*)

CHICK

Ruth, tell this clown I'm okay!

RUTH

No, no, Officer—he's all right!

EILEEN

Yes, John—you can let him go now.

LONIGAN

(*Disgustedly*)

Ah!

RUTH

Oh, thanks, Chick! Eileen, I can't believe it! Look, it's a press card! I've got a job—I can go to work!
(*They embrace.*)

EILEEN

Ruth, that's wonderful!

VALENTI

What is this—a night club or an employment agency?

VOICES

Come on! Sing it! Let's hear her sing!

VALENTI

Come on, what are you cryin' for?

EILEEN

I'm happy!

RUTH

We're both happy!

VALENTI

Well, I ain't! And the customers ain't! Sing or blow!

RUTH

She'll sing! Go on Eileen—

EILEEN

I can't—I can't just stop crying and start singing!

RUTH

Of course, you can!

EILEEN

Do it with me, Ruth, please!

RUTH

In front of all those people!

VALENTI

Come on! Come on!

EILEEN

Ruth!

RUTH

Should I, Mr. Valenti?

168

WONDERFUL TOWN

VALENTI

Sure! Do something—do anything!

RUTH

All right! Play the band—the "Wrong Note Rag"!
(RUTH *and* EILEEN *stand up.* RUTH *explains the routine.*
RUTH *and* EILEEN *hurriedly whisper directions to each
other during the announcement.*)

VALENTI

Folks, something new has been added. Another glorious
voice joins us. The Wrong Note Rag— Hit it, boys!
(*There is an old-fashioned blaring introduction and*
RUTH *and* EILEEN *march forward and perform the number they have known since their early childhood. They
work in a dead-pan sister-act, style circa 1913.*)

RUTH AND EILEEN

Oh there's a new sensation that is goin' aroun'—
Goin' around— Goin' around— Goin' around—
A simple little ditty that is sweepin' the town,
Sweepin' the town— Swee—eepin' the town—
Doo—Doo—Doo
Doo—Doo—Doo—Doo—Doo—Doo
They call it the wrong note rag!

It's got a little twist that really drives ya insane,
Drives ya insane, drives ya insane, drives ya insane,
Because you'll find you never get it out of your brain,
Out of your brain— Ou-Out of your brain!

169

Doo—Doo—Doo—
They call it the Wrong Note Rag!
(*The music and the girls' spirit and energy become in-
fectious and the crowd joins in.*)

ALL

Bunny Hug!
Turkey Trot!
Gimme the Wrong Note Rag!

GIRLS

Please play that lovely wrong note
Because that wrong note
Just makes me
Doo—Doo Da—Doo, Doo—Doo—Da—Doo, Doodoo!

That note is such a strong note
It makes me

EILEEN

Rick-ricky-tick rick-ricky-tick tacky.

RUTH

Wick-wicky-wick wick-wick-wick wacky.

Don't play that right polite note
Because that right note
Just makes me
Blah-blah-bla-blah, blah-blah-bla-blah blah blah!

Give me that new and blue note
And sister
Watch my dust,
Watch my smoke
Doin' the Wrong Note Rag!

> (*They break out into a corny ragtime dance, and the couples at the Vortex, loving it, pick up the steps and join them, building the number to a high-spirited finish. There is wild enthusiasm from the Vortex patrons as* RUTH *and* EILEEN *hug each other happily.*)

VALENTI

Well, that's what drove 'em out of Ohio. What are you gonna
do for an encore?

EILEEN

Encore? Did I get one?

RUTH

Of course you did! You were terrific! Go on!

VALENTI

What's it gonna be ?

> (EILEEN *whispers,* "It's Love"! *She goes upstage and all face her.* RUTH *sits on a step downstage.*)

For an encore our little premier donna is gonna get nice and
mellow— Keep it low, folks.

> (*The music to* "It's Love" *starts and* EILEEN *sings—all eyes on her. She is in a spotlight—and so is* RUTH, *watching her.*)

EILEEN
(*As she sings*)

It's love! It's love!
Well who would have thought it.

(BAKER *enters, looks about, sees* RUTH, *he goes to her and
touches her shoulder. She turns, shushes him and turns
back to watch* EILEEN.)

If this is love
Then why have I fought it?

(RUTH *does a take as she realizes it is* BAKER, *but she
shushes him again. This time he takes her in his arms
and kisses her. Still dazed, she pushes him away, saying,
"Ssh!" Then suddenly realizing what is happening, she
turns back to him and rushes into his arms.*)

What a way to feel—
I could touch the sky.
What a way to feel—
I have found my guy.

BAKER
¡Holding RUTH, *as all turn to watch them,* EILEEN *beaming
happily at them across the club*)

It's love at last,
I've someone to cheer for.

RUTH

It's love at last—
I've learned what we're here for.

WONDERFUL TOWN

ALL
(*Singing*)

I've heard it said,
"You'll know it when you see it."
> (RUTH *and* BAKER, *holding hands, oblivious to everything
> but each other.*)

Well, I see it— I know it—
It's love!

> (*The curtain falls*)

CPSIA information can be obtained at www.ICGtesting.com
Printed in the USA
LVOW132335051012

301755LV00007B/158/P